THROUGH THE FIRE

By Mary Lynn Case

*"...Fear not, for I have redeemed you; I have called
you by your name; you are Mine. When you pass
through the waters, I will be with you; ...When you
walk through the fire, you shall not be burned, nor
shall the flame scorch you."*

Isaiah 43:1,2

Through the Fire
ISBN 0-88144-225-9
Copyright © 1996
Second edition, 2005
Mary Lynn Case

Published by
Christian Publishing Services
P. O. Box 701434
Tulsa, OK 74170

Cover Design: Bob Simpson
Text Design: Lisa Simpson

Dedicated

to the memory of our sisters,
Carol Ann Harlow
and
Jane Anne McBride
and to my husband,
Don Case,
whose love and encouragement
and living example
made this book possible
"This is my beloved, and this is my friend."
Song of Solomon 5:16

For information or to order books:

Don or Mary Lynn Case
9708 Whitney Court
Granbury, TX 76049
(817) 573-0080
donmlcase@aol.com

Contents

I

Through the Fire

In 1989 my husband's sister Carol was diagnosed with ovarian cancer. She fought valiantly against the disease for four years before her death in April of 1993. It was during this time that I first began searching the scriptures about divine healing. I wrote out the scriptures with comments for Carol so that she would be encouraged. These scriptures and notes on praying for healing are found in the last part of the book.

Little did I realize at that time how the Word would come back to minister hope to us in other crises. Later my own sister was diagnosed with lung cancer and died in November of the same year that Carol died. During the week of my sister's death, my husband was in the hospital undergoing surgery for cancer of the ureter.

After believing the doctor's report that he had "gotten it all," we were surprised to learn three months later that Don had two fist-sized tumors outside the bladder with invasion of the bladder. Later it was also discovered that the cancer had metastasized to his lungs.

The truths that I had found before still held true. In addition, we discovered more about God's grace and love as we walked through this new fire. It was these three experiences that led to the writing of the first edition of this book. Only God knows why some people are healed and others are not. However, what other people learn in their trials can often be revelations for others going through similar trials.

In 2000 I was diagnosed with breast cancer and have gone through surgery and chemotherapy. During this time (starting in August of 2000), I read over the first writing of this book several times to recall to my mind what God had taught us before.

In one of his sermons, David Wilkerson says that people need to recall the miracles from their past to enable them to walk through new crises. In the Bible, God instructed His people to remember His miracles as encouragement. As I faced my personal crisis, I was encouraged once more by the promises of God.

It is our hope that God will use our experiences to shed His light on the truths He chooses to reveal to each person who reads this book. I pray that our sharing of these experiences will bring encouragement and hope to people walking through the fires of their own crucibles.

As I begin to write my story and to add to this second edition, we are again facing a crisis situation. Our precious daughter, Beth, who is thirty-eight years old, was recently diagnosed with this dreadful curse of cancer. Believe me, it is much easier to deal with a disease that wants to destroy your own life than it is when your child is involved. More than ever we know that only a merciful, loving God and Father can get us through this traumatic experience.

Once again we find ourselves clinging to the promises of God and to His hand as we walk through still another fire of this dread disease. We pray to come out of the fire refined and molded more into the image of our precious Lord and Healer, Jesus Christ. He is our Source, our Strength, our Peace. To Him be the glory as He sheds His healing power upon Beth and upon us.

"Blessed be the God and Father of our Lord Jesus Christ, the Father of mercies and God of all comfort, who comforts us in all our tribulation, that we may be able to comfort those who are in any trouble with the comfort with which we ourselves are comforted by God" (2 Corinthians 1:3,4).

II

OUR FIRES
Part 1

CAROL, JANIE, AND DON

That April day of 1989 all of the family members were together at the hospital for Carol's surgery. We reminisced and shared. We cried together, prayed together, even laughed together (as families do to ease the strain of the difficulty of waiting). We waited all day to hear some word, hoping for the best and dreading the worst. Then it came: "It is cancer."

Shock, dismay, disbelief, fear. All of the classic emotions ran rampant in that group of loved ones as we heard the dreaded diagnosis. Carol's surgery had been only partly successful. They had removed some tumors but had to leave other cancer cells and masses. Her prognosis from the doctor was five years.

As it turned out, Carol, my husband's sister, lived exactly four years longer after the original diagnosis. They were years in which she valiantly fought to live every day to its fullest. She underwent four more surgeries and many hospital stays due to either the cancer itself or to the side effects from the treatment.

Carol worked through her fears and her questions and overcame many obstacles that would have devastated other people with less courage or with less support. The years she fought saw her family by her side, pulling together in love to help her carry the load until the end. Throughout those years we again cried together, prayed together, shared and laughed. Many precious memories were built and bonds were forged in ways they had not been forged before.

My family went through the same traumatic experience in September of 1992 when we discovered that my sister, Janie, had lung cancer. By the time it was discovered, it was in Stage IV with metastasis to her brain. The doctors said that she could have as short as three months to live. She lived for fourteen months.

At the same time we entered Janie in one hospital in Amarillo, Don's sister Carol was in another hospital across town, dealing with more complications from her cancer. This set the standard pattern for our lives for the next several months. We spent much of our time going back and forth between towns and between hospitals to see about and to care for our sisters.

My husband, Don, spent much of his time in Amarillo with Carol, even staying at night with her. While he ministered to her in so many ways, he saw what cancer and the treatment of cancer can do to one's body. With the special gentleness that he has and with his keen insight into a woman's feelings, he anticipated her needs and met them in ways that led her to describe him as "Knight Don of the house of Case, ever my hero." The closeness they'd always shared grew during this time as Big Brother took his turns by her side.

Even when Carol was having to stay in Hospice during the last weeks of her life, all of the family experienced poignant, memory-filled moments. These moments included a gamut of emotions from joy to pain. Each of us had very special times with Carol, and all of us will always remember these cherished times in our hearts.

One funny experience during this time was the conga line. Don, his brother (Mike), Mike's wife (Karen), and I were taking Carol around the hospice grounds. One of us was wheeling her in the chair while another dragged the IV line behind it. It seemed that all of us thought at the same moment about how we must look; and falling behind each other in line, we began the conga dance. The nurses there loved it. Carol acted embarrassed and protested, but all the while she was laughing so hard that she began to snort, a habit we have always teased her about. It had been a while since she had laughed like that, and we praised God for the snorts!

A more solemn occasion occurred on Easter Sunday when Don served communion to all present. We used crackers for the bread. The nurses loaned us pill dosage cups, which we filled with cranberry-strawberry juice. The people taking the communion included Catholics, Episcopals, a Jewish man, and members of several Protestant groups. We were truly ecumenical, and we felt God's blessings on our endeavor. It was a moving occasion that touched all of us deeply.

In April of 1993 Carol's battle ended, and she released her struggle to rest in the Lord.

The Sunday before she died, Carol asked us what color the sky was; and we felt that she wasn't inquiring about the real sky. This was validated later when she opened her eyes and said, "It's so beautiful....so beautiful!"

Earlier during her illness, Carol had told me of her fear of dying. Therefore, I remarked, "See, Carol? You didn't need to be afraid at all."

"Yes," she replied. "That was really dumb of me to be frightened."

And then very softly she said, "Jesus is here."

I told her that He had come to take her home.

Since Carol is an artist, it seemed so appropriate that God would choose the beauty and colors of His paradise to show her what awaited her.

When she left us a few days later, surrounded by dear friends and family, we knew that she was "running to be with Jesus" as our younger sister, Melissa, was encouraging her to do.

Carol was able to share her love and appreciation to all those who meant so much to her (her dear friends and her family, including nieces and nephews). She wrote short notes of gratitude and praise or advice to each one individually. These notes were read at her funeral. What a blessing those words were to each of us!

In the meantime, my sister Janie's treatments with chemotherapy and radiation were ongoing. Although she went through some difficult times, she also had some wonderful days of energy and joy. The Lord renewed her love for her home and for her husband, John, in a very special way and brought the two of them into a closeness they had not had before. I know that John treasures those days of closeness as my sister did. I could see God working in so many ways to show Janie how He had blessed her. She became aware of how many people loved her as her friends rallied to her side to help in every way.

She and John were able to celebrate their thirtieth anniversary with a wonderful trip to Dallas to be with their three beautiful daughters and other family members. She had never seemed happier than when we drove them to the airport. Her illness brought her a new awareness of and perspective on life. This in itself was a miracle.

A couple of months after returning from Dallas, Janie was told that she had to have more radiation on her brain. These treatments really began to sap her energy, and we could see her growing weaker and weaker. When the tumors did not respond to the radiation therapy, Janie struggled more than she had before both physically and emotionally.

That summer I would ride my bike over every day and try to get her to walk. At first we'd go a little further each day. However, eventually we ended up just sitting on the porch and rocking. We had always teased about all the things we'd do when we were "little old ladies." Suddenly we were doing them way too soon! I will always treasure those last, bittersweet days we shared together.

Janie was hospitalized with pneumonia a couple of weeks before her death. One night I told her how proud I was of how hard she had fought. She asked, "Do we keep on fighting?"

She had shared with a good friend that no one knew the struggle she was experiencing, so I felt that she was extremely tired and really wanted my permission to just let go. I told her that I would fight with her as long as she wanted me to, that I could never be ready for her to go, but that I would quit fighting and release her when she was ready.

Later during that time she said she felt, "weird...like I'm in two different worlds...like walking in a catacomb."

I asked her if maybe it was because she was soon going on to a different world, and she replied that maybe it was.

"Well, Sister," I asked, "how do you feel about that?"

Looking me straight in the eye, she answered in her strong, deep voice, "Just fine!"

So I knew that she felt that her fighting was at an end and that she was accepting that.

* * * * *

I believe that it is very important for loved ones to be sensitive about the feelings of the person who is in the midst of the struggle. When it becomes obvious that the person has reached the point of surrender, those of us who will be left behind must be willing to release that dear one to God. Sometimes this must be done out loud to the person, letting that one know that although we will miss him or her terribly, we "give permission" for entrance into a glorious new life. Other people have shared this with us before, and we found it to be true in our own situations.

I was so touched as I sat on one side of Carol's bed and her mom sat across from me, holding Carol's hand. She told her daughter, "I'm here to hold your hand until Jesus comes to take it. Then I'll let go and put your hand into His." She had come to accept that Carol was preparing for a new home far better than any she could have on earth and was willing to give her child back to her heavenly Father.

I have known of dying people hanging on to this life and going through much unnecessary suffering because someone they loved dearly was not willing to let go. Then when they felt released by their loved ones, they died soon after, leaving their pain and agony behind.

We have to yield our will to the will of the one in the struggle between the desire to live or to die. When that one has shown that he is himself ready to go on and has gotten to the end of his will to continue the fight, we must accept it and be totally unselfish in our reaction, relinquishing him to go on to be with God.

Revelation 21:1-27 describes the New Jerusalem. Verse 4 says, *"And God will wipe away every tear from their eyes; there shall be no more death, nor sorrow, nor crying. There shall be no more pain...."* Verse 5 says, *"Behold I make all things new."* Verse 27: *"But there shall by no means enter it anything that defiles...."* Chapter 22 tells of the River of Life and trees of **healing**.

Therefore, disease has no part in heaven. When we release our loved ones to go on into that glorious kingdom, we are releasing them from the bonds of affliction and suffering that can never touch them again.

17

We can be comforted as we picture them in newness of life in such a kingdom as this. Our sister Cindy comforted Carol with this picture of heaven. She reminded her that there was no cancer where she was going.

* * * * *

Since I had to go to Amarillo to be with Don during his surgery, our Aunt Bea came to take care of Janie during the last week of her life. Auntie is an LVN, and she and Janie always had a very special and precious relationship. We will be ever thankful to her for being there when we needed her the most.

Auntie's family and ours have always been close. Her son, James, and daughter, Nancy, and their families were all so supportive and loving to my sis during her illness. She told me often how much they meant to her.

I was also so grateful that our son, Mark, and our daughter, Beth, had already made plans to be in Pampa for that time and were with us when we lost Janie. Their presence was such a comfort to me and to the other members of our family. Beth was so precious to hold on to me and to watch over her dad, who returned from the hospital the day before Janie's funeral. Mark took care of his grandmother and was a source of strength for his three cousins.

Before Janie left us, all three of her girls had very special private times with her. Her oldest, Leslie Lynn, told her: "Mom, you'll always be here to me. Every time I teach, you'll be in that room. I'm a teacher because of you."

For weeks before Janie died, Mary Lisa seemed to be able to anticipate Janie's needs and was so supportive and helpful in every way that she could find. Several times she had stayed at nights by her mother's side, sometimes sleeping on the floor. Janie seemed to really look to her and to depend upon her in a special way.

Lee Anne, our baby, spent the last night of her mother's life curled up in the hospital bed with her. She sensed that the end was near and felt as I did that her mother shouldn't be alone when the time came. This time I slept on the floor. Both of us were able to say "Good morning" to Janie one more time on earth before she went on into the most glorious morning of her life—-her first morning in God's heavenly kingdom!

What a legacy Janie left behind in these precious daughters!

When she finally breathed her last, she was surrounded by all those who loved her best. Our dear mother knelt at the end of her bed, her heart broken.

Watching our mother have to face the loss of her firstborn child was heartrending for us. Our dad had gone on to be with Jesus in 1970, and we knew that Janie and Daddy would be together. But it was still such an unnatural situation when Mother and I walked up together to the funeral home to see Janie. Neither of us had ever dreamed that we would one day share this experience.

Mother had always been able to find some way to help her child, but for the first time in her life she didn't have the power to take away or to ease her pain.

Still she was comforted by knowing her child's final destination was with a heavenly Father who loved her even more than she did.

* * * * *

Losing a child must be the most difficult of all losses. But what joy must accompany that loss when a parent knows that she has instructed her child in the faith that led her into heaven! Sorrow must be doubled when those left behind are unsure of the destination of the one who has left them.

Although our sisters were not healed from cancer, they both gave us assurance of their destination before going on to be with the Lord. As Christians we need to remember that even though they were not victorious over the cancer, they did not lose. For a child of God a terminal illness is a "no lose" situation. Even in death there is victory, a secure place of eternal glory in heaven, where there is no disease.

> *"Where, O death, is your victory? Where, O death, is your sting?"*
>
> 1 Corinthians 15:55 NIV

* * * * *

My husband's battle actually began two months before we finally knew that he, too, was fighting this disease of cancer. The first day of August 1993, I was at the church, working for the back-to-school outreach.

This was the first fall that I had not gone back to school myself since I had retired that spring after teaching for thirty years. Don had decided to take early retirement from his job and had accepted a position as administrative pastor of our church. This job was to begin in two weeks. We had given up a long-awaited dream of moving to Colorado and were in the process of selling our property there and rediscovering our own little town of Pampa, Texas.

Then came the call that began the next lap of our journey. The secretary came to tell me to get to the hospital. Don had been rushed there on an emergency from his workplace. I had no idea what to expect when I arrived, and I prayed all the way.

Arriving at the emergency room, I found Don very pale and in intense pain. The doctors were relatively sure that he had a kidney stone blocking his left ureter. When he didn't pass a stone during the night, they proceeded to do emergency major surgery, which included opening him up and going through his bladder.

After the surgery the doctor remarked, "Whatever it was disintegrated when I got there. There wasn't even enough left to send to the lab." At the time I didn't even think about how this sounded. Looking back later, I wondered why some surrounding tissue was not sent at the time.

Don began recovery from this surgery and started working at the church. He began experiencing more and more problems until finally on October 20 (on the same day my sister was admitted to the hospital with pneumonia) the doctor who did the surgery decided to do a cystoscopy. They then found suspicious tissue and sent it to the lab.

The next morning the doctor came in to tell us the bad news: Don had a malignant tumor in his left ureter. From the beginning Don's remark and his attitude was, "Honey, that word *cancer* does not scare me. Our God is bigger than cancer." Knowing what we had just experienced with our sisters, I knew the kind of faith that this statement showed. God had taken the seeds of belief in divine healing that Don had planted into his heart, and He was releasing the power of that Word to bring forth the faith that Don would need to go through this trial.

After I left the hospital, I fell apart emotionally. I immediately called my precious friend Cathy to enlist her prayer support and her encouragement. Cathy and her husband, Karl, have always been prayer warriors for us, often at God's urging when we haven't even talked with them. They are always sensitive to our needs. Her first response to me was, "Whose report will you believe?" And we agreed together to believe God's report, which I had previously researched and studied. I knew that it was in God's will for us to pray for healing for my husband. The seed of faith that had been implanted was budding forth into my heart, too.

Cathy and I also agreed together that God would protect us from any negative reports that might try to come to us. She prayed that God keep away those who could not speak life into us at this time. I believe that His faithfulness in protecting us from our own negative thoughts and from the negative words of others really kept our hope intact.

* * * * *

This is an important lesson for everyone when circumstances seem overwhelming. I suggest that you and another Christian agree in this same prayer of protection. As God's Word tells us: *"Pleasant words are like a honeycomb, sweetness to the soul and health to the bones"* (Proverbs 16:24) and *"A merry heart does good, like medicine, but a broken spirit dries the bones"* (Proverbs 17:22). To keep your spirit from being broken and having it affect your health, keep only the joy and the hope of pleasant words and of God's Word in your heart. Refuse to listen to negative thoughts or to negative speech from others.

Make it a point to fill your life with joy. Remember that the Bible tells us that a happy heart is healing. Our sisters' senses of humor added joy and happiness even up to the last days. Even in the midst of sadness, this joy gave us strength.

In addition to this scriptural admonition, even in the medical profession physicians agree on the benefit of joy in the healing process. Many studies have been made on how laughter and joy can actually aid in physical healing in a person by releasing endorphins, natural mood-boosting chemicals, into his body.

These endorphins help build the immune system and can reduce pain. They also create or build the infection-fighting antibodies. Studies show that the benefits of laughter include better blood circulation and improvement of cardiovascular problems, relief of problems in the digestive system, lowered blood pressure, and increased oxygen consumption to reduce respiratory problems. [See Norman Cousins' book *Anatomy of an Illness* (New York: Bantam, 1981), and *Fifty-two Simple Steps to Natural Health*, Mark Mayell and editors of *Natural Health Magazine*, Pocket Books, Simon and Schuster, Inc. New York, NY, 1995).]

* * * * *

Our church family came to our side during this time. It was through this wonderful family and other close Christian friends that our hope began to be rebuilt. They were so faithful in their praying, even getting up in the night to lift us up and to seek God's words for us. Their prayers and their words of life to us prepared us for what was to come, although at this time we had no idea of what lay ahead.

Their words of wisdom can be used by anyone going through a time of discouragement. Therefore, I want to share them with you throughout this book. Although every situation is unique, there are basic truths that we can learn from each other and apply to our own lives. Some of what was shared with us at this time may speak to your own heart.

Over and over we were told that God would go with us and would be glorified in the final results. This became truth. Although cancer attacked Don's body, God used this to build Don for his ministry. He is a strong, comforting minister for those in pain. He has a special anointing to minister to people in the hospital or in similar situations.

God can use anything we walk through to bring us into a better place to carry on his work. Remember: *"...the sufferings of this present time are not worthy to be compared with the glory which shall be revealed in us"* (Romans 8:18).

Even children shared. Karl and Cathy's daughter, Karli, sang a song and told her mother that it was "for Pastor Don." That song brought so much comfort:

"Great is Thy peace
I'm taught of the Lord.
Great are His promises
I have in His Word.
I shall be glad
And not be afraid,
'Cause Jesus takes care
Of the things that He made."[1]

One place we went for comfort was to the home of our dear friends Jane and Ronnie. They both had words for us. Ronnie said he kept getting one word, "Rest." He said that he believed that God would have us to rest in Him and to rely on Him during this time. Jane said that she was receiving, "Under your feet." She gave us the scripture Romans 16:20: *"The God of peace will crush Satan under your feet shortly."* Both of these words were confirmed over and over.

Ronnie's word of resting in God was confirmed at once. Later on the same night that Ronnie gave this word, Don and I were in bed. He was lying on his back with his arm around me. We were talking when he said, "Honey, I can't feel you or the mattress or anything. It is as though I'm floating in air, but I can feel two hands holding me up by my back."

God was holding him up to show him that he was indeed in His hands and could rest in His care. What a loving God we have!

This lesson of resting in the Lord was one of the new concepts that God showed us in our own walk that I had not discovered in my study of the scriptures previously. Later on this spoke more and more to our spirits.

The Sunday night following the new diagnosis of cancer, the soloist at church sang "You Are Defeated." This song says that whatever you want to say to the Prince of Darkness, you are to write it all down on the bottom of your feet. This will remind Satan of his position as far as you are concerned.

Because of Jane's earlier word about Satan being under our feet, Don wrote I AM (God's name as He gave it to Moses) on the bottoms of his shoes to remind Satan that he was under God's feet and under ours. Every time Don crossed his legs, we were reminded of Satan's position and of our position over him in Christ.

During this same Sunday night service the pastor of our church prophesied that Don would have a healing ministry. When he said this, it was like a shot of electricity went all through Don's body. He had his hand on my shoulder, and I felt it jolt through him.

Later the evangelist's wife said that she saw Don as a pillar for the church, and for a pillar to be strong, it has to go through the fire. "Going through the fire" became a recurring theme for us.

While we were being encouraged, we also were concerned about having to break this news to Don's mother. Knowing what she had just gone through with losing a child, we worried about the effect this news would have on her. We began praying for God to build up her faith to believe with us for a miracle, knowing how hard this might be under the circumstances. We began praying God's peace to encompass the entire family as it had encompassed us.

Having lost all confidence in the local urologist at this point, we elected to go to Amarillo, a nearby town, for further treatment. The new doctor ran all kinds of tests and found that Don not only had a tumor but also had lost function of his left kidney. He performed an operation to remove both the ureter and the left kidney. Thus Don had his second major surgery on November 1, only three months after his first one.

While Don was in the surgery the following scriptures ministered to me as I sat in the chapel, praying for strength and peace:

"He shall give his angels charge over you...In their hands they shall bear you up" (Psalm 91:11,12). I prayed for God's angels to assist in the surgery. Angels are *"ministering spirits sent forth to minister for those who will inherit salvation"* (Hebrews 1:14).

"The steps of a good man are ordered by the Lord, and He delights in his way. Though he fall, he shall not be utterly cast down; for the Lord upholds him with His hand" (Psalm 37:23,24). I prayed that Don would feel God's hands holding him even as he felt Him before.

I was reminded that *"our light affliction, which is but for a moment, is working for us a far more exceeding and eternal weight of glory, while we do not look at things which are seen, but at the things which are not seen"* (2 Corinthians 4:17,18).

I also re-read all of God's words to us before and was reminded to "believe the report of the Lord."

Again our dear church family was there for us to keep our spirits lifted. Those back home dispatched angels to the operating room and kept us lifted in prayer. Those in Amarillo with us took turns staying in the chapel during the entire surgery. They sang, shared scripture, loved us, and just held me when I

27

needed human touch. Our dear friends Jerome and Beverly never left the chapel. During all the days ahead Beverly and Cathy became Aaron and Hur for me, "holding my hands up" when I was too tired to fight the battle on my own. Their prayers were constant. (See Exodus 17:10-12).

It was a long, long day for all of these friends and for all of the family members who kept vigil. They came for him at 12:30, and we didn't hear anything definite until about 8:00. The doctor's report after the operation was that he believed that he had removed all the malignancy.

When we finally heard from the doctor that Don was okay, our friends and family joined hands to praise and thank God. We filled the waiting room! In addition to his coming through the surgery successfully, we had other specific prayers that were answered: no nose tube, no blood transfusions, no ICU!

Don's brother stayed with me until they brought Don to his room. Off and on during the next week John, our youngest brother-in-law, would come and help Don walk and just visit and love on us. It felt so good to have others step into the role of "big brother."

Brittany, one of the young girls in our church, made Don a poster to put on the wall of his hospital room. It was decorated with her hand-drawn Peanuts characters and with scriptures on healing. The message on it declared: "We Believe the Report of the Lord!" This message became our "motto" during the rest of our trial. Even when the devil tried to use our sisters' deaths to discourage us, we held on to what we had from God's Word.

Don had many visitors, words of encouragement, and gifts during his hospital stay. Steve Rogers, a minister friend of ours, came from Plainview to share with Don. Steve had a miraculous cure from cancer, and the Lord quickened in him to share with Don and to encourage him. He reconfirmed that what was meant for evil, God would turn to good.

Don returned home the day before we buried my sister. He went to the funeral with me and, even in his weakened condition, was a rock for me.

Gradually his strength returned, and Don and I began to lead what we thought would be a "normal, routine existence." Since then I have decided that *Normal Is Just a Setting on Your Dryer* is more than a book title.[2] It is true to life!

For the next four months several times I awoke in the night with a word from God in my mind and in my spirit. (I've joked that when I am asleep is the only time that I am quiet enough for God to get through.) Every one of these messages was supported by one or more persons; and looking back, I know that they were God's way of preparing us for what was ahead.

The first time I awoke with one word in my mind: RESTORE. Just that one word. I had a dream that I can't remember, but that word just sank into my mind and my heart. I believed it to be God's promise as to what He was going to do for us. At the time I wrote in my diary: "Maybe 1994 will be our year of restoration."

* * * * *

Incidentally, I recommend keeping a journal or a diary during your crisis times. In times of discouragement you can be lifted up when you can read of God's faithfulness in the past. As the song says, "Hasn't He always come through for you? He's the same now as then. You may not know how; you may not know when. But He'll do it again."[3]

* * * * *

The next word I received in the night was, "KEEP FOCUSING ON JESUS." Often in trials we tend to lose sight of Him. Our flesh demands attention on our circumstances. When we deny our flesh and keep our eyes on Him and our hope on His promises, our walk is filled with peace that is impossible otherwise.

A poem by B. J. Hoff says:

When answers fail to come, don't be discouraged.
Keep leaning on His steadfast love
And trusting in His will.
For knowing why won't really make a difference,
But growing close and knowing Jesus will.
(Source unknown)

Seeking the Giver is more important than seeking the gift and should be our true desire. Regardless of the outcome of any situation, having Him as the center of our lives will make us victors. Jesus as our focus was reiterated several times during the next year.

On another night in November (in the middle of sleep again), God impressed me to read two books from the Old Testament, *Nahum* and *Habakkuk*. I **knew** that had to be from God because on my own I would not have chosen these two minor prophets to read. Again God confirmed His Word to us.

Nahum 1:7: *"The Lord is good, a STRONGHOLD in the day of trouble; and He knows those who trust in Him."* Our God is a place of safety in trouble.

Nahum 1:15: *"Behold on the mountains the feet of him who brings good tidings, who proclaims PEACE."* The Hebrew word for peace is **shalom**, which means completeness, wholeness, peace, **health**, **rest**, harmony.

Nahum 1:12,13: *"Though I have afflicted you, I will afflict you no more; for now I will break off his yoke from you, and BURST YOUR BONDS apart."* God is able to break the bondage of cancer off this family. My prayer is for this yoke of cancer to be taken from us and from future generations.

Habakkuk 2:4: *"The just SHALL LIVE by his faith."* *Shall live* comes from the Hebrew *chayah*, meaning to live, to flourish, to enjoy life, to recover health.

Habakkuk 2:9-11 These verses describe what Don refused to do. He did not build his life by the world's standards of success but on God's standard, giving up his retirement dream and instead becoming a minister for His Father.

Habakkuk 3:18: *"Yet I will REJOICE in the Lord, I will joy in the God of my salvation."* Regardless of outward circumstances, we will not allow the devil to steal our joy. The importance of keeping joy in the midst of circumstances was one lesson that was proven to be true again and again in all three cases (Don's, Carol's, and Janie's). Again we were reminded that *"the joy of the Lord is your strength"* (Nehemiah 8:10).

Habakkuk 3:19: *"The Lord God is my strength; He will make my feet like deer's feet, and He will make me walk on my high hills.*" We will rise above the circumstances.

In December God's word was SECURE. In February a friend gave us this scripture: *"But whoever listens to me will dwell safely, and will be* SECURE *without fear of evil"* (Proverbs 1:33).

This last word came after a day in which Don and I had shared that we were both feeling anxiety about his coming checkup. The devil seemed to be using our sisters' experiences to bring out fear of the cancer. We chose to stand upon His promises to us through His word and through His Spirit to our spirits. We determined again: "We will believe the report of the **Lord!**"

I prayed as did the father in Mark 9:24: *"Lord, I believe; help thou mine unbelief."* I found that God honors even this smallest prayer of trust and of obedience. Our peace returned.

When we went in for Don's checkup on February 8, the doctor found some inflamed tissue inside Don's bladder. He decided to do a biopsy a week later. We went by the church in Amarillo, and one of the ministers there repeated the words "secure" and "God's rest." He also said for us to draw near to God's presence and into His light. Any darkness from Satan cannot follow us there.

On February 15, the day of the biopsy, we stood on the promise that God is *"a rewarder of them that diligently seek him"* (Hebrews 11:6 KJV). It would be a while before we saw this reward; and before it finally came, we still had more struggles to go through and more rivers to cross.

When the doctor returned to the room after he had done the biopsy, he was very disturbed and told me, "It is very bad...very serious. There was more malignancy in the bladder. I got it, but it is invasive. We need to keep him overnight and later take an MRI to see what is there outside the bladder."

I wept and wept. I couldn't bear the thought of Don going through any more pain or another surgery. Again our wonderful church family was there. Ronnie just held me and cried with me. The tears just kept coming.

Don's overnight turned into four more days in the hospital with high fever and bladder spasms and infections. That first night of the hospital stay, Don was asleep. I left the room and went to a little waiting room down the hall. I just became overwhelmed by everything. I cried out and wept and had an anguishing emotional turmoil. I experienced what has been called "the dark night of the soul."

Never had I felt such hopelessness. I was fearful of losing my dearest friend and beloved companion. I was confused about God's plan. Satan bombarded my mind with every negative thought possible.

Don was going to die! I would be all alone at a time when we had planned to spend our golden years together. God hadn't heard our prayers after all.

I felt totally alone. I could physically feel my heart breaking as a sharp pain pierced through me. It was as though a dark cloud was in the room, and I couldn't even pray. Finally I just started saying, "Jesus, Jesus, Jesus."

It worked! Just the power of His precious name brought calmness and peace and overcame the dark thoughts and the fear and the despair.

The cloud lifted.

Praise Him and bless His holy name. "There is strength in the name of the Lord; there is power in the name of the Lord; there is hope in the name of the Lord."[4] How true those words became to me that night!

In my weakness, He was made strong (2 Corinthians 12:9). If you are ever to the point of hopelessness and cannot seem to be able to pray, remember this simple truth: Jesus' name is a fortress, a comfort. His name makes the devil and all his insidious thoughts disappear.

I still felt a need to hear a voice. I needed what our dear Lou calls "God with skin on." I had never felt so totally alone. The one who usually comforts me was in a hospital bed and needed comfort himself. I called Don's sister Cindy, and we cried together and shared together.

Cindy remarked, "This game would be easier to play if we just knew what quarter we were in."

"Yes," I replied, "but we do know Who the Coach is!"

After we talked, I felt better. I went back to Don's room and got my diary. I sat out in the hall by Don's room, re-reading what God had given me. And I re-read David Wilkerson's newsletters. Cathy, our night nurse, came by and prayed with me. I finally found rest and peace and went to bed.

The next day a friend of ours came by. He reminded me about Jesus in the Garden of Gethsemane. Even the Son of God looked for comfort from other men in His agony. Again let this encourage you to find others to be with you.

That night the Crawfords and the Andersons, two couples who are close friends, came over. Linda ministered to me so much, reminding me of God's Word and of His promises and the Truth. Gail ministered through her love. I could see her sharing my pain with me as she looked at me with those loving eyes filled with tears. Once before I asked Gail, "What would I do without you?" and she answered, "You'll never have to know." What a precious lady my friend Gail is!

Praise God for Christian friends—-no, for brothers and sisters in Christ! They are more than friends. I will be eternally grateful for the wonderful support of all our brothers and sisters in the Lord.

* * * * *

If you are going through a traumatic situation, a loving group of people is vital. They can intercede when you are too exhausted even to pray. They can remind you of God's promises during your weak times. They can just hold you and cry with you. They can help care for you physically, emotionally, and in ways you won't even think of.

If you do not have anyone to help you go through your battle, I strongly recommend that you find a church family to be your support group. Even if you do not know the people closely, you will find that Jesus can form lifelong bonds in a very short time. One of the biggest blessings to come out of our traumatic experiences was to be given newfound friends in Christ. During that time we developed friendships that will never be broken with people who had been only acquaintances. They became like family to us.

Actually Christians are all "blood kin" anyway. We are all kin because of <u>the blood of Jesus</u>. Praise God for this kind of relationship! *"There is a friend who sticks closer than a brother"* (Proverbs 18:24).

* * * * *

Lori, a young lady in our church, had been led of God to 2 Chronicles 20. She said that God spoke that scripture for us and for our church body.

The next morning I wanted to read this passage to Don, but the only Bible in the hospital room was a New Testament. So I went to get our car Bible. We read about Jehoshaphat and claimed his promise, prayed his prayer, and believed that we would receive the same answer that he did.

<u>Our stand and His promise</u>: v. 9— *"If disaster comes upon us,...we will stand before...Your presence...and cry out to You in our affliction, and You will hear and save."*

<u>Our prayer</u>: v. 12— *"O, our God,...we have no power against this great multitude that is coming against us; nor do we know what to do, but our eyes are upon You."*

<u>Our hope</u>: v. 15— *"Thus says the Lord to you: 'Do not be afraid nor dismayed because of this great multitude, for the battle is not yours, but God's!'"* (Another translation says, *"The battle*

36

depends on God, not on you.") Again God was telling us to rest in Him.

V. 17— *"You will not need to fight in this battle. Position yourselves, stand still and see the salvation of the Lord, who is with you...Do not fear or be dismayed; tomorrow go out against them, for the Lord is with you."*

V. 20— *"Believe in the Lord your God...believe His prophets, and you shall prosper."*

The result: v. 30— *"...his God gave him* REST.*"*

Right after we read it, I looked at a sermon note that I'd stuck in this Bible sometime in the past. It confirmed the message for us: "The Lord wants to fight your battles for you. God can defend His children." Other notes that I had written in the Bible at some unknown time in the past also spoke to us very clearly how this passage was appropriate for our situation.

It was as if God saw to it that we had that particular Bible. Don and I always said that we wished God would send telegrams to us. We felt as though He **did** this time.

We got call after call reporting how the home groups had prayed for us and lifted us up and were encouraged. Every one of them had some word that this would not result in death, that Don's time was not yet, and that his ministry would be completed.

One night during his hospital stay, I was staying with Don's parents at their home in Amarillo. Before I went to sleep, I asked God to show me what was ahead. Since He had been speaking to me in the middle of the night so often, I asked Him to reveal in my sleep what we were facing. I realize now that all the previous words had been preparation for what was to come.

Early in the morning I was impressed that the tumor was not contained in the bladder but was massive and outside. I woke myself up screaming, "No, God, no!"

Just as clear as an audible voice, in my spirit God said, "Can't I take care of that too?"

And my spirit and I both said, "Yes, Father, You can!"

I got up to see the time so that I could compare notes if God had spoken to Don at the same time. Then I went back to sleep—good sound sleep that only can come with God's peace. No fear at all! I truly had God's peace *"which surpasses all understanding"* (Philippians 4:7).

I didn't share this with Don because God hadn't spoken it to him yet. I just kept it and "pondered it in my heart."

We went home on Saturday, and that Sunday in church the pastor had chosen 2 Chronicles 20 for his scripture! God was making sure we got it! Chris, a young woman who had been healed of cancer, shared her testimony. In it she told how she had prayed over the chemotherapy before it entered her body, asking that it attack only the bad cells and not the good ones. We would use this advice later.

Oma Lee and A. D., two dear saints of God, gave Don Psalm 118:17,18 and faithfully stood on it for Don. *"I shall not die, but live, and declare the works of the*

Lord. The Lord has chastened me severely, but He has not given me over unto death."

Later the Lord gave us: "*And you would be secure, because there is hope*" (Job 11:18). He was repeating His earlier word of **secure**.

> **Secure**: to hide for refuge, to trust, to be confident, to be sure, to be bold (confident, secure, sure), to hope

> **Hope**: expectation, live, thing that I long for

On February 22 Don had the MRI, and on February 25, Dr. W called to tell us the results. The day he called, I was alone at home. My spirit was restless and disturbed (the devil trying to take away what God had promised), and I was praying for God to instill me with His assurance.

God's peace is not something we can take for granted. Our flesh and Satan will continue to try to snatch this peace away. This precious gift must be guarded diligently. We do this by staying in God's Word, remembering His promises, and praying. Having His peace is worth whatever it takes to keep it. It is the most powerful stronghold we have for protection in the floods and fires of life.

As I prayed to God for a return of the peace He had given to me, the phone rang and the doctor began telling me that there was a large mass outside the bladder. As Dr. W told me the really bad report, God began calming me and assuring me. I asked the doctor to call Don at the church, and then I drove there. All the way God ministered His faith to me more and more. I **knew** God would heal Don. God gave me the gift of faith to trust Him for this healing.

Arriving at the church, I found Don pretty shaken. I shared with him what God had revealed to my spirit that night at his parents' home. The pastor and his wife came and prayed with us and cried with us.

God's peace came back. We declared: "No matter how big it gets, our God is still bigger than cancer."

It was at this time that God began burning a new impression into our hearts. Don was drawn to the story of the three Hebrew children. He was stirred by their attitude when they declared to King Nebuchadnezzar in Daniel 3:17,18: *"If we are thrown into the blazing furnace, the God we serve is able to save us from it, and he will rescue us from your hand, O king. But EVEN IF HE DOES NOT, we want you to know, O king, that we will not serve your gods or worship the image of gold you have set up"* (NIV).

Don KNEW God was able to heal him of cancer and was believing that He would. Yet in his belief he was also willing to surrender what he desired unto God's plan for him. If he had to walk through the fire of chemotherapy or another surgery or whatever God willed, Don said, "You do it Your way. I trust You completely."

* * * * *

In nearly every instance of divine healing of people whom I know personally, one consistent pattern seems to hold true. The healing came after the person was willing to trust God's highest good and SURRENDER totally to what God had planned and how God planned to use his experience to work for his good. As long as a person refuses to fully trust, he is limiting what God wants to do.

What we truly believe about Who our God is determines our ability to trust Him completely. If we KNOW in our hearts that He is all-wise, is good, is kind, and is in love with us, then we act on that. We trust Him because we know He will do what is best for us. When we can't see His plan or His purpose clearly, we can always trust His heart.

In Isaiah 43:1,2 God promises to be with us when we pass through the waters and when we walk through the fire. He doesn't always take us out of the fire, but **He always goes through it with us**. Regardless of why we have to walk through the fire (because of our own disobedience or because of a satanic attack or whatever), the fire will serve God's purpose of refining us in a way that only He can. He will be faithful to see to it that ALL things *"work for the good of those who love him, who have been called according to his purpose"* (Romans 8:28 NIV).

* * * * *

Don had a needle biopsy on the mass to determine what kind of cancer he had. When we talked to Dr. W later, he was more disturbed than we were as he told us the bad findings. Our peace from God was intact. We understood what "surpasses all understanding" truly means.

This peace remained intact even when we had a conference with an Amarillo oncologist who told us that there were actually <u>two</u> masses outside the bladder, one by the bladder and the other extending toward the rectum. It seemed the news just kept getting worse.

We both read David Wilkerson's sermon on Hezekiah from 2 Kings 18,19. In this passage Hezekiah received a letter from Sennacherib, representing Satan, the god of this world. When he received the letter, Hezekiah *"went up into the house of the Lord, and spread it before the Lord...and prayed"* (2 Kings 19:14,15 KJV).

David Wilkerson suggests in the sermon that we, too, often receive letters from the devil in the form of divorce papers, pink slips, X-rays, and with these "letters" we receive the devil's jibes and taunts:

"So you believe Jesus heals, do you? Well, where is He now? Why do you still have to suffer? You gave Him everything, and look what happened. He gave you nothing but continued suffering in return...."

Wilkerson goes on to tell us how to react to the devil's accusations:

So what do you do when you are confronted with a message from the devil? First, you have to spread the enemy's letter before the Lord, as Hezekiah did...

Pray and seek the Lord. Don't ever talk or reason with the devil. Simply hold your peace, as the people in this passage did with the taunting messenger: "The people held their peace, and answered him not a word: for the king's commandment was, saying, Answer him not" (2 Kings 18:36 KJV).

...God takes your letter personally. He said, "Devil, you didn't send that letter to My child. You sent it to Me!"

...He who touches you touches the apple of God's eye. God says His loved ones are safe and that the devil

cannot harm them." (2 Kings 19:32,34 KJV and Psalm 34:7 KJV).[5]

The Lord impressed both of us individually to follow Hezekiah's example. We took the x-rays and reports and laid them and ourselves before God. Don and I prayed over them and told the Lord to return them to the sender—POSTAGE DUE! We refused this report from Satan, delivered through man. We believed God's report as seen in His Word.

As we began seeking God's will for Don's treatment, we prayed for God to bring the same comfort and peace to our children as He had to us as they, too, tried to work through this bad news report. Both of them were very close to both their Aunt Carol and their Aunt Janie, whose losses were still new; and we knew the agony and fear that they could be going through. We prayed for God to give them the same faith to believe with us for a divine healing.

Yes, we prayed for God to <u>give</u> them the faith they needed. This was another lesson that we were learning. Faith is a gift from God. It is not a quality that we can work up in ourselves. This truth became real to me when I read a marvelous book by Charles S. Price, *The Real Faith*. (This book has been recently republished under the title *The Real Faith for Healing*.)

As he puts it:

> *One thing I do know, and that is, I cannot produce faith. Neither in me—nor in you—are there the ingredients or qualities which when mixed, or put together, will make even a mustard seed of Bible faith. If this be true, are we not foolish to attempt to bring about results without*

it? If I want to cross a lake, and find there is no way to reach the other side, except by boat; would it not be foolish of me to struggle to get across without a boat? The thing I should seek is the boat—not the other side of the lake! Get the boat, and it will take you there.

There are certain things which we receive by faith and only by faith. There is not the slightest ambiguity regarding that in the Word. Rather it sets forth a clear declaration of the truth. Now where do we get the faith which will take us across our "lakes"? The answer to this question is positive and sure! Between the covers of the sacred Book there is mention made of faith as the gift of God and faith as a fruit of the Spirit. Whether it be gift or fruit, however, the source and origin of faith remains the same! It comes from God. There is no other source of faith; for it is the Faith of God!

...You can't have faith without results any more than you can have motion without movement.... As we need the gift or fruit of faith, it is imparted by the Lord, in order that God's will, rather than ours, will be done on earth, and in us, even as it is in Heaven.

...All things are possible to them that believe. But it is important what you believe. To believe that you, apart from grace and divine impartation, are the possessor of a power that can remove mountains is dangerous indeed. I know many who have tried such a program in their own strength, and perchance on the basis of self-righteousness, but sorrow has been their lot, instead of joy.[6]

This lesson became more and more real to me as we went on. It was obvious that in myself I could never have the kind of faith that I did for Don's healing. In myself the circumstances and the medical diagnoses would have been devastating. Only God could supply me with the depth of faith that I was experiencing. However, as Charles Price explains in his book:

> In the development of His will in your life, let me assure that when faith is needed, it will not be withheld; for the Giver of every good and perfect gift is the Author and Finisher of our faith.[7]

This kind of faith is available to all of God's children.

We had seen advertisements for the Cancer Treatment Centers of America in some magazines and on television. We had discussed finding out more about them when a dear Christian gentleman, Gene Durkee, called to say that he felt we should look into CTCA as a possibility. God was letting us know His direction again through confirmation by a Christian friend.

I called and found out that there was a Cancer Treatment Center in Tulsa, Oklahoma, and we made reservations to go there and look it over. We learned that they emphasized nutrition. I had been reading Anne E. Frahm's book, *A Cancer Battle Plan,*[8] which discusses the role nutrition plays in cancer. We were convinced that it would be vital to Don's health for us to follow wise nutritional guides. I had already talked to a nutritionist in Lubbock, and Don had started taking a regimen of vitamins.

We were also glad to learn that the center offered Christian programs and had Christian psychologists on staff as well as chaplains. Their approach to treating the whole man (physically, nutritionally, emotionally, spiritually) was what we were looking for.

After we prayed about it, we made reservations to fly to Tulsa. We knew that if God was not indeed leading us there, He would put up red lights for us and we would know.

There were no red lights!

A very caring gentleman picked us up at the airport, and we visited about the Lord on the way to the hospital. Once we arrived there, all of the people who met with us were just wonderful. The atmosphere and spirit in the hospital and in the staff brought us peace, joy, and hope.

The nurses in the clinic had sweet Christian spirits. We could tell that they desired to truly minister to the patients. During the times we went there, we really became close to this precious group of women. We also developed a valued friendship with the mother of one of the young women in our church. This darling lady, Marsha Eaves, was an angel to us as she helped us in every way she could in her capacity as Patient Services Representative at the hospital. Although now in another position there, Marsha continues to unselfishly help us in every way she can. What an angel!

We consulted with four different doctors: an oncologist, a urologist, a radiologist and the doctor who would be our head physician to co-ordinate the others. They made the decision to run more tests to be sure that we did not have any more "surprises" ahead of us before deciding on treatment.

Before the tests were run, the urologist suggested doing radical surgery. He wanted to remove both of the masses and the bladder and put in a uriostomy. He felt that with this surgery Don would have three to five more years to live. Neither of us ever felt any kind of peace about this further surgery.

The results from the tests they ran took any decision away from us. The findings showed metastasized cancer in the lungs. Surgery was out of the question until chemotherapy had been tried. As the doctor explained to us, "This is more in God's hands now than in ours."

Don replied, "It always has been."

Even after finding out this added discouraging report, our peace and our faith did not waver. We were so thankful to God for these two gifts of faith and peace, recognizing Him as their one and only source. Nothing else but God's Spirit in us could have given us such emotional comfort at this time. Nothing that we had in the natural realm could have brought forth these feelings.

Of course, the doctor, Don, and I all agreed that God can use man's knowledge to help toward healing. The sculpture of two hands that were once in front of the hospital represented God's hand and man's hand working together to heal. The three of us prayed together and asked for divine healing and divine wisdom to choose our course.

Afterwards we met the psychologist there. He, too, was most encouraging and agreed with us that God is still in the healing business. He and his wife are both on staff there and are such encouragers. Their gentle spirits really reach out to the patients as they help them to work through all of the emotions involved in this kind of treatment. They both gave wonderful comfort.

During one visit with the psychologist he gave us Romans 5:1-5 and Romans 8 to meditate on. He also discussed Hebrews 12:1,2 with Don and reminded us to stay focused on the Healer, not on healing. This confirmed what God had dropped into my heart before: "Keep focusing on Jesus." Dr. Ellison is still a good friend and a source of encouragement for us.

While we were at the center, more vitamins were added to Don's original plan that he had already started, and we learned more about nutrition through informative sessions and lessons taught by the nutritionists there. We also discovered another book that gave more information about the importance of diet and vitamins in cancer treatment: *Beating Cancer with Nutrition* by Dr. Patrick Quillan, formerly on staff in Tulsa.[9]

We believe that the center holds out hope that other places don't give. Most of the patients who have been elsewhere agree that CTCT is the best place to be. Even though the staff members don't claim that everyone will be healed, they do focus on and try to give each patient a quality life for whatever time that patient does have left. As I have already mentioned before, one way they do this is by their whole-man approach, treating physically, nutritionally, emotionally, and spiritually.

* * * * *

I advise everyone going through any kind of illness to carefully and prayerfully choose a hospital or treatment center that offers hope and that employs people who care about the patients in a real way. Find a treatment center whose staff sees and treats the patient as more than just a patient, but as a person with other needs to be met at the same time.

* * * * *

One vital way that CTCT differs from other cancer centers is in the method of administering the chemotherapy. They give the chemo in fractionated doses. This means that they give the same regimen of chemo that other hospitals use but in smaller doses over a longer period of time so that a patient's system is not "zapped" so hard. The side effects are minimized when the dosage is administered like this, approximately one week each month. In comparing the traditional treatment of our sisters with Don's, we can see how much better fractionated dosage is. I would recommend the center for this reason if for no other.

The center uses many other methods, adjusting the treatment to each individual patient. God led Don to be treated with chemotherapy. God used Don's experiences with taking chemotherapy to bring him to an understanding of what this experience entails. He is, therefore, able to relate to and encourage others going through this difficult treatment. Don's drug treatment has enhanced his ability to minister to other cancer patients.

We went for five days each month, starting in March. Our first oncologist, who was the one who was there all during Don's chemo treatment, was a dear man who carried his stethoscope in one pocket and a prayer book in the other. The new oncologist is another precious man who has great compassion for his patients.

We were also blessed with Christian nurses and aides who would pray with us and who would share their faith with us while we were going to the hospital regularly. One night three of them came into Don's room for what he described later as a "real prayer meeting."

I do not want to leave the impression that the treatment center is connected in any way with a Christian organization. It is a hospital run for profit like all others. However, there are many people on the staff who truly live their beliefs. Part of the commitment statement says that "we are committed to honoring God through our beliefs and actions." The Christians on staff do this successfully. I know of at least three times when the nurses led a patient to the Lord before that patient died.

Don and I remembered the testimony of Chris, the young cancer survivor in our church, and we prayed over every drop of chemo before it went into his body. One time Don was in a panic when he thought it was going in before we had prayed and yelled, "Hurry, Honey! It's starting to drip!" Sometimes the nurses prayed over it with us. We asked for the chemicals to attack only those cells that they were meant to attack and for God to protect the good cells.

Don's side effects from the chemo were minimal, especially when considering the strength of the four different drugs included in his treatment. He did lose his hair, but he was a very handsome "baldy." He looked like a combination of Jean Luke Picard and Yul Bryner! When I told him that all of the women up at the center thought he was still cute, he remarked, "Yeah, but they're all bald, too!"

He always tried to "make the best of a bald situation." (Sorry for the bad pun.) When our daughter wanted pictures to see her dad without his hair, Don posed as Jean Luke Picard, as a Moonie, as a "Hairless Krishna" and as a kung foo artist.

When we later flew to Philadelphia, our daughter met her dad at the airport in a full-headed mask of a bald-headed woman. Like father, like daughter! After she saw her dad, Beth didn't want him to grow hair after the treatments ended because she liked him so much without it. (Beth has said that she is upset because the treatment she will have won't cause her to lose her hair, and she really wanted to wear wigs and have fun with it. Obviously, she already has the sense of humor part down well!)

Another side effect was extreme tiredness for a couple of days toward the end of the week after each treatment. Even this did not cause him to lose a full day of work. A few times he would work only half a day on those days, but that was all. He never had nausea or vomiting.

The chemo did cause nerve damage, resulting in numbness in his legs; but he is learning to adjust and live with it. The doctors are not sure whether or not his feeling will come back; but if it doesn't, it is not a bad trade off. Don thinks of this numbness as a constant reminder of what God has done for him.

When we went to the hospital, we ate in the common dining room that is a part of the patient floor. The architectural design has the patient rooms in a horseshoe around a large gathering area divided into two sections. One is a "living" area with a television, a piano, couches and chairs. On the other side is the dining room, where patients and their families can eat together and share together. The doctors often come by and sit down to eat and to visit with the patients rather than shutting themselves off.

Some of the best therapy goes on in these gathering places, where people facing the same crisis can share and encourage and help each other. During this time bonds of friendship formed that were unlike any others. We grew close to several of the patients and their loved ones. We saw evidence of many of the other patients drawing together, too. We became especially close to one man and his wife and even drove to Michigan to see him before he died. We still stay in touch with his wife.

Often on our visits there I would play the piano. Others would come by and sing. One young man always brought his guitar and his Beatles music. I'd TRY to play with him. We really had some "jam" sessions! This homelike atmosphere brought all of us closer and made us feel that we were all fighting the same battle together. This is so much better than a regular hospital, where the patient remains in his room and often feels that he is fighting all alone.

Most patients are only hooked up to the chemo several hours during the day, so the patient is free the rest of the time to do as he pleases. The doctors had a hard time finding Don in his room at times because he would take the chemo at night and we would run around and go to the park and around Tulsa during the day, usually taking some of the other outpatients or members of their family with us. The patients who cannot go away from the hospital can be seen walking around the pretty grounds, some dragging their IV poles along with them. Not the typical hospital setting!

Of course, going to any hospital every month is not like taking a vacation. We did have times when we dreaded the trip and times when we wondered if our lives would ever be "normal" again. But many blessings came from these trips. We both felt that God used us to help other patients there. Don's attitude, his faith, and his witness were encouragement for the others.

Our family in the Lord remained a constant source even while we were gone. We were lifted up in prayer; Karl "stood in" for Don at a healing service at our church; and our dear brothers and sisters in the Lord sent cards and called while we were away. Some of them even came to Tulsa to check on us. One of our good friends from Ft. Worth sent his sister, who lives in Tulsa, to come and take us on a guided tour of the city. We **never** felt alone.

These trips back and forth each month continued from March until November. After three treatments they ran tests again in June. We were sitting at the breakfast table and visiting with the oncologist when he got a call. Soon he came back to tell us that the metastasized cancer in the lung was gone; one of the fist-sized tumors was gone; and the other one had shrunk to walnut size! We were overwhelmed and so grateful that God had begun His healing work so quickly.

Don had two more chemo treatments, more tests, and the results in August showed no sign of cancer! So after **five** treatments and much prayer, his Stage IV cancer was gone!

This came as no surprise to my husband. Earlier in the week before we went back in August, I asked him what he felt in his spirit about the report we would get. He said, "They won't find anything."...And they didn't!

At that time the oncologist cut the chemo by 25 percent and set up three more treatments to be sure to get rid of any residual cancer cells. After that we would return for periodic testing.

The results of the tests that were run to show that the cancer was all gone were given to us on August 1, a year to the day when Don went into the hospital with the first signs. On the anniversary of that awful day, we were celebrating!! We took that as a sign from God to reconfirm His healing grace.

Don had his last chemo in October, and we went back for him to be tested in November. All of the tests were clear again. They took out his port, the surgical implant for administering chemotherapy, and set up our next visit for three months later.

The urologist (the one who had wanted to do the radical surgery) couldn't believe it when he examined him. He remarked, "Mr. Case, do you realize that this type of cancer just doesn't respond to treatment like this so fast?"

Don answered, "It does when Dr. Jesus is on your team."

One of the chaplains remarked that he didn't understand how any self-respecting cancer would invade Don Case's body in the first place. He said that it should go and find someone with a negative attitude if it wanted to be successful.

One of the doctors admitted that Don's case was a miracle, which is not a very usual remark for a medical person to make. His exact words: "Don, you are a walking miracle. Jesus healed ten lepers, and only one returned to thank Him. I know you will be that one" (Luke 17:12-19).

Don did indeed have a heart of gratitude for God's awesome gift of healing. He shared as often as he could, and many people called us to find out about his healing. Some heard about him from friends and wanted to find out about the hospital and his treatment. We always included God's hand in the process and tried to be used the way God wanted to use us.

We did still have times of weakness. Prior to our going back for the tests in February, the devil really tried to do a number on Don. He sent doubts into his mind about his healing.

I could tell that he was despondent and asked him to open up to me. He told me that he was having doubts. Satan was saying, "You're not really healed. What makes you think God healed you? Who do you think you are? This is just an act."

When Don finally confessed this and asked for prayer from a few of our faithful prayer warriors, our Father sent His faith to replace the doubt. By the time we went to Tulsa, Don was feeling positive again.

The scripture we got this time was about when Satan asked to sift Peter and Jesus said, *"Simon, ...Satan has demanded permission to sift you like wheat; but I have prayed for you, that your faith may not fail; and you, when once you have turned again, strengthen your brothers"* (Luke 22:31,32 NASB).

When God brought this scripture to my mind, I discovered a new truth: Jesus did not pray that Peter's **flesh** would not fail, but that his **faith** would not fail. Jesus knew that Peter's natural man would be unable to stand against his own fear and against the accusations hurled at him. Knowing that Peter's flesh was weak, Jesus prayed that Peter's faith would not fail him and that **when** (not **if**) Peter turned back in faith, he would become a tower of strength for his brothers. This was indeed Peter's destiny.

As with Peter, Jesus understood that Satan was sifting us and that our flesh was weak and our doubt strong, but God was sending forth His faith to us once again and strengthening us. Jesus was praying for us, too. Jesus is still interceding for His people, sitting at the right hand of God, the Father (Romans 8:34). Jesus understands our human doubts and weaknesses.

Satan had been sifting Don. However, just like Peter, Don had Jesus (now at the right hand of our Father God) praying for him. We put the devil on notice that he might have permission to sift us, but our Jesus was praying for us, and we were holding on to His promise. Again we were filled with His peace.

Sure enough, the reports again showed "No carcinoma" on all of the tests. This has been the finding on each visit we have made since the first one.

God has been magnified through Don's healing. Don consistently gives the glory to Him for the healing and the thanks to the faithful doctors who aided Him with their knowledge. As people continue to call him for questions about his healing, he always includes God's part and witnesses to His healing power and grace. He has used his experiences as Jesus told Peter to do in the scripture above: to "strengthen (his) brothers."

We pray that we NEVER take this healing gift for granted. We pray to be worthy of God's grace and goodness to be used by Him as He wills. We know that God has a plan to be fulfilled out of all of these experiences and what we have learned from them, and we look forward to the fulfillment of that plan. To Him be the glory!

III

OUR FIRES
Part 2

MY STORY

Upon learning that I had been diagnosed with breast cancer, several of my friends suggested that another book was in the making. I gave this idea some thought and even decided on a title: *Mammograms at Half Price and Other Silver Linings*. Since we decided on a second printing of *Through the Fire*, I have instead added my story to Don's. (Incidentally, I do get a discount on my mammograms, and I found other silver linings behind this cloud of cancer.)

My experience began in August of 2000, when I finally decided that the lump in my breast might be serious. Since I have fibrocystic disease and some lumpiness is always there, it took me awhile before I was concerned. However, this time it seemed different.

By the time I went to the doctor to find out if I was indeed feeling something wrong in my breast, the cancer was large enough that there was no question that I might indeed have a malignancy. My gynecologist and the physicians who did the mammogram and sonogram all gave us a sense of urgency. In less than two weeks from the first exam, I went in for a biopsy.

God's hand through all of this became obvious from the very beginning. I was able to get a biopsy almost instantly. The surgeon had an opening on the following day after we visited with him. Don and I went to lunch, discussed this, decided to go ahead and prepared for immediate surgery.

Because of problems I've had in the past with surgical procedures, we also began to pray for specific answers to take care of those problems: that the IV would be a simple procedure and that a vein would be easy to access; that I would be completely under the anesthesia before I was wheeled down for the surgery; and that the anesthesia would not make me sick.

All three of these prayers were answered. The girl who did my IV was great and got it on the first try after she and I prayed together. I had no swelling or pain at the site.

The second answer brought forth our first funny experience. We were reminded of the vital role that humor played in our past trials. When I told the anesthetist's assistant that I didn't want to be awake when I left for surgery, he told the nurse, "Give her another shot of that." That is the last thing that I remember; but Don says that soon after that I slurred out, "Twinkle, twinkle little star" like a drunk. I have no idea where that came from. I'm just thankful that I didn't embarrass myself more. Anyway, it gave Don a chuckle and let him have a moment of laughter even in a serious situation.

Finally, I woke up in recovery with no nausea and in full clarity of mind. This was the first surgery I've ever had where this happened. Of course, my Don was by my side. The first question I asked was, obviously, "Is it cancer?" He told me that it was, and that the surgeon had done a lumpectomy, not just a biopsy. He had also taken surrounding tissue and sent it all to the lab.

This is when my first miracle began to happen. I had no fear come over me at all. From the very beginning God engulfed me with His incredible peace. I never had one single moment of being afraid during the entire time from that first moment until today. Don't misunderstand. My experiences were not a "walk in the park" by any means. I went through every other emotion possible and was on an emotional roller-coaster much of the time; but the one emotion that never took hold was fear. To me, this absence of any fear was a true miracle that God gave to me during this time.

I had to fight back with the Word of God when the enemy tried to send other negative messages and thoughts, but God was so faithful to replace them with hope. He surrounded me with that wonderful peace that only He can give.

I knew that it was His peace because in and of myself I could not have faced cancer without fear. It was as though God was saying to me as He said to Paul in 2 Corinthians 12:9:

My grace is enough; it's all you need.
My strength comes into its own in your weakness (The Message).

God's strength, never my own, was enabling me to face what lay ahead without fear. I will forever praise and thank God for this gracious gift.

God also gave me a remarkable recovery from this first surgical procedure. Four hours after I went in, I was on my way home, feeling very good. I was amazed at how well I did and thankful that God was showing me that He was in charge and would prepare me to face anything that might be ahead of us.

Two days later we went in for the doctor's pathology report from the tests and from the surgery. When I asked questions as to what the long medical diagnosis meant, I found that I had an aggressive breast cancer that tends to metastasize or recur and that there was some involvement in the lymph system. As my questions were answered and the diagnosis became even more serious, I still felt very calm and unafraid. Leaving the doctor's office, we immediately made plans to go to Cancer Treatment Center in Tulsa for my treatment.

During the same time that I was going through all of this, we had to put my little mother in a nursing home, which is the hardest thing I have ever had to do in my entire life. I spent days literally grieving over this. Mother had lived with us for nearly two years and had been a source of joy for us. I hated to have to admit that I could no longer care for her and have her as a daily part of our lives. God was so gracious to lead us to a place where Don's stepsister Frances worked. She was so wonderful to look in on Mother and to help us. We didn't even know she was there until after Mother had been admitted, but having her close helped us to relax and to feel more secure about Mother. Having to leave her was easier since Frances was there, and we knew we could count on her.

God also helped Mother to adjust to her situation. A few days after she was admitted, our friends went to see her, and Mother told them that I couldn't take care of her since I had cancer so she had found this nursing home herself and told us to put her there. I know that God had helped her to decide that she was in charge and that this was best. This eased the situation for all of us. (Mother lived until January 2003, when she went on to be with Janie and Daddy. She was ninety-six.)

After we arrived in Tulsa, we had the usual days of consultations, tests, discussion of treatment choices. The adjective "overwhelmed" best describes how I felt at this time.

During our final consultation with the oncology surgeon, we discussed all of the choices. The three of us then prayed together. Don prayed as we all held hands. After the prayer, the doctor kept my hand in his, looked me in the eye and said, "I want to assure you that I never do anything without asking for the Lord's help. They are my hands, but He uses them."

I cannot explain the feeling that I had rush over me when I heard these words. We already had total confidence in his reputation as a surgeon, but now God had let us know that He would be guiding the surgeon and the surgery.

The oncologist who would be in charge overall was the same precious, caring oncologist who was following Don's case. He would be prescribing meds and following up on my treatment and future testing. After a visit with him, we were about to leave when he hugged me.

I hugged him back and told him that I had all the faith in the world in him. He pointed up at the sky as if to say, "and in Him." I was overjoyed to know that I would be in the hands of two Christian doctors. As in Don's case, Dr. Jesus was the head of our medical team.

After consultations, research, discussions, and prayer, our final decision was a mastectomy and the removal of all the lymph nodes and then chemo. I knew that this decision was the right one to make, but I also knew that this radical treatment would not be without consequences. I was saddened at the prospect of losing my breast; I was concerned about the possible effects of the chemotherapy; I wasn't sure how long the recovery would be or how I would react to all of the invasions to my body or what my emotional state would be.

However, the possible consequences of any other decision were more severe. I certainly didn't want to put my life in jeopardy or to have higher possibility of a recurrence. I wanted to enjoy the "sunset" years with my precious husband and enjoy my wonderful children and my grandboys.

Three oncology nurses at the hospital confirmed that we had made the right decision. All three assured me that with my diagnosis I needed to be aggressive in my approach. I felt at peace about our decision.

We returned home for three days to get ready to return for the surgery. At this time we were on staff with a ministry outside of Azle, Texas. The other people involved with the ministry really covered us with prayer and encouraging words. We also received many E-mails and cards and calls from our friends. I had support from people from my childhood, from our newest friends at the ministry, and from every phase of my life in between. I felt so loved.

We returned to Tulsa on September 6 with surgery scheduled for the next day. We took family pictures, posters, plants and special "treasures" and books to help give me the feeling of home. We determined to make the best of the situation. The night before the surgery I had a very good night of sound sleep with no anxiety at all. God's peace was intact. This blessed peace never left me as I was wheeled into the operating room.

The surgeon removed all the breast tissue, a very thin layer of muscle tissue and twenty nodes under my arm. He inserted my port for the chemo infusions. Afterwards he reported to Don that I had done well throughout these procedures.

During the surgery, Don was supported by our dear friend Stan Cosby, who had once been our pastor, and by other friends whom we had met in Tulsa, Kay Linda and Kendra. These two women had been part of the nursing team that had ministered to Don when he was going through his treatments. They both always left us feeling joyful and hopeful. We felt so blessed to have these special people with him.

The recovery time after the surgery was slow and full of setbacks and discouraging times. As is often the case after surgery, I would have a good day and then a bad one. This is where my emotional roller-coaster ride began. One day everything would be looking up, and the next day I'd hit bottom again. I remember hoping a few days after the surgery that I would wake up and find out I was dreaming. I had adverse reactions to some of the pain medication, which made me feel nauseated, dizzy, and spacey; the drains didn't always drain as they should; the nerves regenerating in my arm created weird, shooting pains; and the exercises I had to start for my arm were painful and difficult. I was discouraged, impatient, self-conscious, and angry. Sometimes for no real apparent reason, I was extremely sad, even to the point of despondency.

However, in between these awful times I would have really good days with energy and laughter. We were so heartened by all of the calls, cards, gifts, and visits. Several people drove long distances to come and check on us. It was during these "up" times that I would remind myself to look forward, past the bad times to when it would be over. I reread the scriptures that had encouraged us before and tried to stay on top on the negative emotions when they came back.

I still wasn't looking forward to what lay ahead of us. I wanted to just skip ahead to when all of the treatments were over.

Even now when I go for tests, one experience that I'd like to just skip altogether is the MRI. I am very claustrophobic; and although they call it an "open" MRI, since they test my brain, they put a contraption that I refer to as an "iron mask" over my head. I had a real panic attack the first time, and since then I have had to be medicated to get through this test.

Through this I learned another lesson about God's provision. Someone advised me that I should be able to depend on God to get me through the MRI without having to take the medication, that I should be able to pray and trust God to get me through my phobia. This idea pushed my "super-Christian" button, and on one trip for tests, I decided to try to do it without medical help. It didn't work!! Then another sister in Jesus told me that God gave the knowledge of the drugs to us, too, and suggested I just be thankful for them. This felt so right to me. After all, I reasoned, I was trusting God as the ultimate healer but still going through surgery and chemotherapy. Wasn't this the same thing? So now I just take the drug, thank God that I have it, relax and manage to get past the phobia involved with my tests.

One of the major traumas that I've had to deal with is the fact that I lost my breast. In the past, before cancer struck me personally, I'd always been stoic about how it would be a "no-brainer" to choose between a breast and a life. However, I found out that in truth this is not as easy to adjust to as I thought it would be. It took me a long time to be able to look at the scar. Each time that the surgeon changed the dressing, I looked away. I wasn't ready to face that particular trauma. I had to fight against the idea that I was maimed.

I decided against reconstruction for several personal reasons. This is a decision that every woman has to make for herself. Although I haven't second-guessed myself about this, it took a long time to get to the place where I came to terms with it. I am able now to joke about looking like Dolly Parton's half sister. I still haven't found a really comfortable prosthesis bra, but I couldn't do that when I had two breasts!

Knight Don of the house of Case has come through for me in every way, just as I knew he would. I am so thankful for my precious, thoughtful husband. I couldn't have done this without him and without God. The primary caregiver has such an awesome responsibility. Those who stand by their loved ones are to be commended. Their role is vital in the recovery process.

Humor and laughter continued to be a part of my recovery. The surgeon's nurse was a delightful lady with a fabulous sense of humor. One time when the surgeon was changing my dressing, he asked her to bring some alcohol and joked that it was for him. She replied, "Well, I could use a drink myself." She also told us funny stories about other cases. She and others helped us maintain our joy in the Lord, which gave us strength. Kay Linda also did her part to always help us find the humor in the situation as did others.

On September 12 the lab reports on the lymph nodes came back. There was no residual cancer, and all twenty lymph nodes were clear!! On our way in to see the doctor, his darling nurse couldn't wait and yelled out to us as we passed her office, "It's a good report!" I feel strongly that the doctors were not expecting this positive report, and I believe that God took care of this for us. We praised Him and rejoiced for another miracle.

In the middle of all of the yucky times that I had after that, I tried to remember the wonderful report and count all of the blessings that I was having. Daily I recovered my strength, and we finally got to leave Tulsa on September 19 and head back home.

I had a few weeks to get Mother completely settled in and to recover my strength and begin a vitamin regimen to build up my immune system. Our friends at Son Shine Ministry were so good to help with food and other practical matters to make things easier. I was so blessed by the outpouring of love from those near and far.

On October 8 we returned to Tulsa to begin chemotherapy treatments. As we had done with Don, we went once a month and stayed several days for the infusions, using the fractionated dosage procedure. Overall I had four sessions of Doxil (a form of Adriamyacin) and Cytoxin. Then I had three sessions of Taxol. These were on an outpatient basis, and we stayed in the hospital guests' rooms.

During these seven months we had fantastic support from loved ones. It seemed that God was nudging someone to get in touch at every point when I might be discouraged. This reminded me of the importance of listening to God's nudges to me about the needs of others. When He brings someone to our minds, we need to act on that remembrance and touch base with the person He recalls to us. So many lives have been touched and blessed and even changed by people being open to God's little nudges.

For the first four sessions, I would go up to the infusion room for five hours after supper, take chemo, go back to the room and fall asleep. This treatment was stretched over five days. The last three sessions I had chemo infusion for four hours for three days of each month. During the hours I wasn't hooked up, we ran around Tulsa and Jenks, a charming little town across the river, enjoying ourselves as we had done when Don was the patient. We are still totally convinced that the fractionated dosage treatment is so much more humane and easier on the body than the standard treatment.

I was very sick on the fourth treatment, but that was due to several contributing factors, which made this session different from the others. Other than that one time, I was never even nauseated. I did find out what Don's sister Carol had meant when she said that nausea from chemo was worse than any other kind. I can empathize with those going through this kind of reaction.

Two chemos I took almost always result in hair loss. I had intended to make the best of it, buy wigs of several colors, and really make Don's life interesting. As it turned out, my hair thinned but never came out, and I never wore a wig. I laughingly called my thinned hair my "chemo hairdo." I believe that God just let me keep my hair as a special favor because He knew I had enough adjustments to make at that time.

In addition to my not-so-glamorous hairdo during this time, I also discovered that I could blame the chemo for other failings. We learned that chemotherapy affects the brain cells and causes some memory loss. Now all of my "senior moments" have become "chemo brain." It's kinda nice to find scapegoats to blame for our human failings!

At the same time that I was undergoing my treatments, in addition to putting Mother in a nursing home, we were building a new home and moving to Granbury. Talk about poor timing!! However, in between treatments I was able to live a busy life and stay up with all of the trips we were taking to check on Mother, with all of the decisions about the house, and with all of the checking and planning involved in building a house. Of course, in November and December we also had all of the holiday preparations and celebrations during that time of the year. We also had to make two long trips. We attended a niece's wedding in Austin and took a trip to Amarillo to check on Don's dad in the hospital. Later, we did all of our packing and moved into our new home the first day of February. Again I was amazed and grateful at how God gave both of us the strength to handle all of this stress at the same time.

In addition to the supernatural strength He gave to us, we found that He was also caring for us financially. We had taken a big loss on our move from Pampa to Azle and from Azle to Granbury, but the provisions we needed were always there. Every time we thought every resource for more funding was used up, God found a new way to replenish our supply. He is so faithful to care for His children!

Don took advantage of the hospital trips to Tulsa to rest up from all the activities we had back home. As for me, I began to feel very spoiled when we went to Tulsa. I had several breakfasts in bed, wore a new pair of jammies every night, and caught up on my reading. One nurse in the infusion room made me her special cocoa every night. I thoroughly took advantage of all of this pampering.

Even though the hospital has really grown since Don went there for the first time, we find that we are still treated with love and care by everyone involved with our program. From the admissions office personnel to the infusion room nurses, the nutritionists, the lab technicians, the people administering the tests, and all of the doctors and nurses involved, everyone makes the patients feel important and cared for. In fact, we arc so spoiled that we find ourselves not having any patience when we are treated indifferently in other places by anyone in the medical profession. A patient needs to be a part of his or her own treatment and should be esteemed by any physician and medical personnel involved.

It has been five years now since my surgery. I have returned to CTCT for all of my follow-up tests, at first every three months, then every six. Now Don and I both go just once a year. In between (at six months) we have blood work. All of the tests have shown good results.

A minister friend of ours told me that this would turn out to be the "greatest thing that ever happened to me." I can't say that I have seen the completion of that prediction as of yet, but I know that so many blessings have come to us as a result of this illness.

As I have already mentioned, our family was reminded of how loved we are. The family of God gave us such encouragement and strength. We saw how Father God could supply whatever strength or other provision that we needed to get through all that we were going through. My going through cancer myself seemed to give more credence to this book. We continue to have input from people from all over the states who tell us how reading about our experiences has helped them in their own situation.

For me personally, this illness caused me to walk more closely with my Father. At the time that the cancer was discovered, we had gone through some very trying times, and I felt totally drained emotionally. In ways I had numbed myself to keep from being hurt again. I was to the point of wondering if I had lost my feelings altogether. God's Word in 3 John 1:2 says: *"Beloved, I pray that you may prosper in all things and be in health, just as your soul prospers."* This illness and my returning to God's Word in a stronger way woke up my spirit, and my soul began to prosper more and more. As that happened, my body responded in a positive way, and my health returned.

Although I know that God did not send the cancer, I can thank God for allowing it to happen because of the blessings that came out of it. I have been reminded that cancer is NOT the "Big C." Instead Christ is the Big C, and cancer is just a little c. The Bible says that at the name of Jesus, every knee will bow. This includes the knee of cancer. This dreaded disease must bow before the Great Physician. I still believe with all of my heart that God is my source and that He will never leave me or forsake me. As the old hymn says, "How I've proved Him o'er and o'er. Jesus, Jesus, precious Jesus, oh for grace to trust Him more."

The Sunday after I wrote the paragraph above, we attended church. One hymn included in the worship service was the one just quoted. I was reminded again of God's intimate knowledge of us. It was as though He was speaking to my spirit that I could still prove Him and trust Him.

We will need this grace to trust Him more and more as once again we face this specter of cancer. The day Beth called to tell us that the melanoma had come back and metastasized to her lung, cervix and lymph system, I was totally devastated. Her words were like hard blows to the gut when I wasn't looking. As she told me the bad news, my internal emotions began to rise up to suffocate me. I could literally feel my heart hurting. I felt a total helplessness, and the tears began to flow. Don went to the other phone to talk to Beth as I tried to get control of my emotions.

I have no idea when I changed position, but all of a sudden, as I grew calmer and could talk to Beth, I realized that I was on my knees. Getting to my knees was not a conscious act on my part at all, but there I was. The Holy Spirit of God within me had taken over the weakness of my flesh and positioned me to receive from Father the peace, strength, and comfort that I would need to talk to Beth and later to face the days ahead.

I still had emotional upheaval in the days to follow. For several days the tears were always there, and each thought of our dear daughter would cause them to overflow. I dreaded what might be ahead for my child as she fought for her life. I was concerned for what the treatment could bring. I had no idea what side effects she might have, if she'd be hospitalized or what. I was concerned about her immune system being strong enough to withstand the treatment.

Her being so far away from us (in Philadelphia) added to my concern and heavy heart. All of the times when I'd kissed the boo-boos, doctored the skinned knees and arms, held her as she cried, explained away slights and hurts, didn't prepare me for a time when I would be helpless to reach her. My longing to hold her and soothe her was almost overpowering. I probably needed to be with her more than she needed me there. Either way, the distance weighed heavily on both Don and me.

Satan, the enemy, would try to use all of these questions, fears, and anxieties to keep us from feeling God's peace and grace. Therefore, I turned again to God's promises. I reminded myself of what He had already done for us. I called the prayer warriors to begin praying. As their prayers went up, His faith came down. God recalled to me His faithfulness in our past experiences with cancer. Hope began to arise in my heart and soul. Our God is sufficient to take care of any circumstance, any trial, any disease, any disappointment, any doubt. Romans 8:28 gives the promise that God can make ALL things work together for the good of those who love Him. He will use this disease to work for Beth's ultimate good and for His glory. I may not know how. I may not know when. But He'll do it again!!

And this is our present prayer— for God to give us grace to trust Him more and more as our daughter has to walk through her fire. We pray that our own experiences with this disease will enable us to minister to her and to build her faith. We ask for His supernatural strength and wisdom and comfort to guide us as we walk once again through the fire of cancer.

We pray that God's hand in Beth's healing will be unmistakable and clear and that Beth will KNOW how much her Father loves her. When we get to the other side of the fire, we pray that her experience of His healing love and power will enable her to be a powerful witness to encourage and bless others.

Recently some dear friends, David and Cindy Hawkins, visited us. As we were praying about Beth, Cindy prayed that the healing that Don and I have received from our Almighty God will be our children's inheritance and that the cancer will not continue to be "passed down." We stand in total agreement with this prayer over our family. May the healing power of the Great Physician pour down upon us and upon our loved ones in Jesus' name.

> *"I shall not die, but live, and declare the works of the Lord. The Lord has chastened me severely, but He has not given me over to death."*
>
> Psalm 118:17,18

IV

PRAYING FOR HEALING

How must we pray for healing?

*"Now this is the confidence that we have in Him, that if we ask **anything according to His will**, He hears us. And if we know that He hears us, whatever we ask, we know that we **have** the petitions that we have asked of Him."*

1 John 5:14,15

Therefore, before God can answer any prayer, that prayer must line up with His Word and His will. So the next question is:

What is God's will as far as our health is concerned?

Let us look at a few passages from the Bible to see what God says about His will for our health:

"...I will take sickness away from the midst of you."

Exodus 23:25

"And the Lord will take away from you all sickness."

Deuteronomy 7:15

"Bless the Lord, O my soul,
And forget none of His benefits;
Who pardons all your iniquities;
Who heals all your diseases,
Who redeems your life from the pit;
Who crowns you with lovingkindness and compassion;
*Who **satisfies your years with good things**."*

Psalm 103:2-5 NASB

"See now that I, I am He,
And there is no god besides Me;
It is I who put to death and give life.
I have wounded, and it is I who heal."

Deuteronomy 32:39 NASB

"Surely He has borne our griefs—sickness, weakness and distress—and carried our sorrows and pain."

Isaiah 53:4 AMP

"He was wounded for our transgressions,
He was bruised for our iniquities;
*The chastisement for our peace was upon Him, **and by His stripes we are healed**."*

Isaiah 53:5

"With long life I will satisfy him, and show him my salvation.

Psalm 91:16

"...for I, the Lord, am your healer."

Exodus 15:26 NASB

"He sent His word and healed them."

Psalm 107:20

OTHERS: Psalm 30:2; Psalm 22:24; Jeremiah 30:17.

All these and others in the Old Testament tell us that God has ALWAYS wanted good health for His people. This same God is the God of today.

New Testament scriptures concerning God's will for our health are numerous. Healing is for US TODAY. Hebrews 13:8 says that *"Jesus Christ is the same yesterday, today, and forever."* What has been God's plan is STILL His plan.

"He Himself took our infirmities and carried away our diseases" (Matthew 8:17 NASB...see Isaiah 53:4,5 NASB).

"And ... a leper came and worshiped Him, saying, 'Lord, if You are willing, You can make me clean.' Then Jesus put out His hand and touched him, saying, 'I am willing; be cleansed' " (Matthew 8:2,3).

Jesus is WILLING TO HEAL! Jesus healed the multitudes, not just a few. He gave His disciples the order and the power to heal the sick. He also gave healing power to the seventy whom He sent out in Luke 10.

Throughout the book of Acts the followers of Jesus had the power to heal. "Gifts of healings" are listed with Christ's gifts to His body, which is the Church today (1 Corinthians 12:9).

Third John 1:2 tells us: *"Beloved, I pray that you may prosper in all things and be in health, just as your soul prospers."* The Bible is God's Word to us today as much as it was His Word in the past, and this is God telling us His will for us: to prosper in our souls and in our bodies.

James gives the Church specific instructions concerning healing. *"Is any one among you sick? He should call in the church elders—the spiritual guides. And they should pray over him, anointing him with oil in the Lord's name. And the prayer [that is] of faith will save him that is sick, and the Lord will restore him; and if he has committed sins, he will be forgiven. Confess to one another therefore your faults—your slips, your false steps, your offenses, your sins; and pray [also] for one another, that you may be healed and restored—to a spiritual tone of mind and heart.* ***The earnest (heartfelt, continued) prayer of a righteous man makes tremendous power available—dynamic in its working*** (James 5:14-16 AMP).

To ask to be healed IS praying "according to His will" as 1 John 5:14 tells us to do. We do not have to say "if it is your will to heal me" because God has told us what His will is. This is explained in the Kingdom Dynamics section of the *Spirit Filled Life Bible*, following Mark 1:45:

How can one have positive faith who begins a request with an "if"? We do not pray for salvation with an "if"...May we not be certain that it is the Lord's will to do that for which He has made redemptive provision? At the same time, one cannot intentionally be living in violation of God's will and expect His promises to be fulfilled. Where biblical conditions for participating in God's processes are present, they must be met; but let us not avoid either God's readiness or God's remedies by reason of the question of His willingness. "If it is Your will" is more often an expression of fear, a provision to 'excuse God of blame' if our faith or His sovereign purposes do not bring healing. If His will is questioned, leave the issue to His sovereignty and remove it from your prayer. Our faith may be weak or incomplete in some regards. We, in fact, may not be healed at times, which should never be viewed as reason for condemnation (Romans 8:1). *Nevertheless, in all things, let us praise Him for His faithfulness and compassion. This is a great environment for healing to be realized and is consistent with the Scriptures, which reveal Jesus as* **willing** *to heal.*[10]

As stated above: *"Where biblical conditions for participating in God's processes are present, they must be met."* For every promise in God's Word, there are conditions. This is not to say that God plays favorites because He never does that. All through the Bible God uses the word **whosoever**, and that means **anyone**. **Anyone** can receive God's promises if he is willing to read His Word and to be obedient to what it says.

WHAT ARE THE CONDITIONS FOR HAVING PRAYERS ANSWERED?

STEP 1:

Be sure to confess all sins before God and make your heart pure as you come into His presence. Psalm 103:3-5 NLT reads: *He forgives all my sins and heals all my diseases. He ransoms me from death and surrounds me with love and tender mercies. He fills my life with good things. My youth is renewed like the eagle's!*

Notice what comes first in these verses. *"Forgives all my sins"* precedes *"heals all my diseases."*

Psalm 103 goes on to explain how God understands our weakness but how His love for us remains forever. Read the entire Psalm and see the glory of God and the power of confession.

The apostle John's prayer in 3 John 2 is for you to *"be in health, just as your soul prospers."* Therefore, getting your soul in the right condition will better prepare you to receive healing. James 5:14-16, another scripture previously quoted, shows the relationship between being healed and being forgiven of sins. It goes on to conclude that not only will you be healed, but you will also be restored in your mind and heart. "Mind and heart" and "soul" carry the same idea in scripture. So we should desire and actively seek soul prosperity.

We need to pray as David did in Psalm 139:23,24 NLT, *Search me, O God, and know my heart; test me and know my thoughts. Point out anything in me that offends you, and lead me along the path of everlasting life.* Pray this prayer as David did with a sincere heart and an open mind. Then, if God shows you anything in your life for which you need forgiveness, deal with it. Confess it before your loving Father. God listens to our confessions, takes our confessed sins and removes them *as far away from us as the east is from the west* (Psalm 103:12 NLT).

Confession and accepting God's divine forgiveness are cleansing. They prepare us to open up to Him as we present our petitions before Him. After we confess our sins, we stand before God clothed in the righteousness of Jesus, not in our own righteousness. Romans 3:22-25 NLT: *We are made right in God's sight when we trust in Jesus Christ to take away our sins. And we all can be saved in this same way, no matter who we are or what we have done. For all have sinned; all fall short of God's glorious standard. Yet now God in his gracious kindness declares us not guilty. He has done this through Christ Jesus, who has freed us by taking away our sins. For God sent Jesus to take the punishment for our sins and to satisfy God's anger against us.* We don't have to depend on our own goodness but just rely on His. How comforting that knowledge is!

In her book *Lord, I Want To Know You,* Kay Arthur warns that sin will affect a person's spirit and this effect <u>can</u> lead to sickness of his emotions and his body. If this should be the case, confession should be the first step toward asking the Father to come in with His healing power.

Even if the sin God reveals to you was not the source of the illness, you have still dealt with a possible wall between you and God. As a result, now your prayers can be more effective, not weakened by guilt or doubt.

First John 1:8-10 NLT says: *If we say we have no sin, we are only fooling ourselves and refusing to accept the truth. But if we confess our sins to him, he is faithful and just to forgive us and to cleanse us from every wrong. If we claim we have not sinned, we are calling God a liar and showing that his word has no place in our hearts.*

Therefore, we are to be honest with ourselves and before our loving, forgiving Father. Take the first step toward soul prosperity and thus the first step toward your healing. Confess any known sin, let God remove it, walk in forgiveness, and go forward toward God's healing grace.

STEP 2:

Abide in Jesus. Unite yourself to Jesus. Let Him live in you. Jesus says, *"If you abide in Me, and My words abide in you, you will ask what you desire, and it shall be done for you"* (John 15:7,8).

Read John 15:5. Jesus tells us, *"Apart from Me—cut off from vital union with Me—you can do nothing"* (AMP). The fruit you bear from being **connected to the vine** is for the glory of God (v. 8). **One fruit can be the faith that leads to healing**.

STEP 3:

Jesus' <u>words</u> must also abide in you. *The Amplified Bible* says, *"And My words remain in you and* **continue to live IN YOUR HEARTS"** (John 15:7). We must have His words in our HEARTS, not just in our heads.

> *"...After those days, says the Lord: I will put My laws in their mind and write them on their hearts."*
>
> Hebrews 8:10

The Bible says that God's words even have the power to heal.

> *"He sent His word and healed them...."*
>
> Psalm 107:20

> *"Unless Your law had been my delight, I would then have perished in my affliction. I will never forget Your precepts, for by them You have given me life."*
>
> Psalm 119:92,93

I love the Proverbs verses that speak of God's words being a source of healing: *"My son, attend to my words; consent and submit to my sayings. Let them not depart from your sight; keep them in the center of your heart.* ***For they are life to those who find them, healing and health to all their flesh.*** *Keep your heart with all vigilance and above all that you guard, for out of it flow the springs of life"* (Proverbs 4:20-23 AMP).

When God's words are *in our hearts*, they become a part of us. Sometimes as you read the Bible, a scripture will literally warm your heart. You will feel as if God is saying to you, "This is for you." When this happens, take that scripture, memorize it (learn it "by heart"), and claim it as God's word to you.

This rhema word from God is what makes your desires line up with His will so that He can answer your prayers. With God's rhema word in our hearts, we can have what the apostle John calls *"the confidence... in approaching God: that if we ask anything according to his will, he hears us. And if we know that he hears us—whatever we ask—we know that we have what we asked of him"* (1 John 5:14,15 NIV).

STEP 4:

When you pray, use the will of God as He has revealed it to you through His Word and **through your spirit** listening to His Spirit. Call upon Him to fulfill His promises for your good health. As you pray, remind God of His promises to you. Recall the scriptures He has put **into your heart** and use them in your prayer. This is not being presumptuous. The Bible instructs us to do this: *"Put Me in remembrance...State your case, that you may be acquitted"* (Isaiah 43:26). And in *The Amplified Bible*, Isaiah 62:6 reads, *"You who [are His servants and by your prayers] put the Lord in remembrance [of His promises], keep not silence."*

Remember all the promises from scripture for good health. Personalize God's promises as you read His Word. Put the name of the patient in where it will fit, or substitute first person pronouns. Claim His promises for yourself or your loved one **after He speaks**

these promises to your heart. Remember that it is in HIS will for you to be healthy.

STEP 5:

Believe that God will answer your prayer **regardless** of what the outside world or circumstances are telling you.

> Jesus says, *"Whatever things you ask when you pray, **believe** that you receive them, and you will have them."*
>
> Mark 11:24

> *"But let him ask in faith, with no doubting, for he who doubts is like a wave of the sea driven and tossed by the wind."*
>
> James 1:6

*"For assuredly, I say to you, whoever says to this mountain, 'Be removed and be cast into the sea,' and **does not doubt in his heart, but believes** that those things he says will be done, he will have whatever he says"* (Mark 11:23). The mountain mentioned here stands for any trial or situation that seems impossible in the human element.

Remember: Mark 11:23 says we must not doubt in **our hearts.** Let the rhema word from God build your faith and keep your faith to believe His promises. The devil will send doubts to our **minds,** but we are to hold on to God's Word in our **hearts.** Believe and profess that belief **out loud** to drive away the devil and the doubts he sends into your mind. Refuse anything the devil tries to send your way.

The Bible says, *"Faith comes by hearing, and hearing by the word of God"* (Romans 10:17). So if you have

Christ's Word in your heart, you have enough faith to trust in it. One Bible teacher, Hugh Smith, puts it this way, "You have faith to do anything you have Word to do." He says that if you've heard the Word, you have the faith.

I would add that you have the faith after the words have been made a part of your heart as discussed in Step 3. Jesus says, *"Let not your HEART be troubled"* (John 14:1). Even if your mind says something else, make it an act of your will to believe in your deep hidden man, the real man (the seat of the will and the reasoning powers). If God has spoken into your spirit and quickened His promise to be yours, hold on to it in spite of what your mind or your circumstances say. I have already discussed the author of this kind of faith previously.

To quote Charles Price again:

That is how faith comes! Not through the channels of human concepts. Not along the paths of human understandings. Not by the abilities of minds to comprehend, or the power of the intellect to affirm. Reach with fingers such as those for the moon and you will struggle and groan in vain to possess it. But let Jesus speak, and the soul is lifted. One little word from Jesus is worth all the words in a dictionary of human language.

There is hope for the blind Bartimaeus of the Jericho Road of today when Jesus of Nazareth is passing this way...and more than hope; for when He hears our cry of helplessness, He will not pass us by...When He speaks, hope is kindled until it becomes a fire that burns away all doubt and

unbelief, and the warmth of a divine and beauti-
ful faith brings healing to the soul.[11]

I was so encouraged when I remembered the words from Jesus that I had received, especially my "one little word" of **restore**.

I encourage you to speak the scriptures aloud. The faith comes by HEARING, and saying the Word out loud just adds to your faith. It strengthens your hope and makes the Word of God seep more into your inner being.

STEP 6:

Diligently seek for God, believing in His goodness. *"But without faith it is impossible to please Him, for he who comes to God must believe that He is, and that **He is a rewarder of those who diligently seek Him**."*

Hebrews 11:6

Again **what you believe about God is impor-tant**. For Him to reward you, first you must believe that he **will** reward, and you must seek Him. A very important reminder: Seeking God is of more impor-tance than seeking healing.

Jesus says in Matthew 7:11 that our Father in heaven gives **good things** to them who ask Him. Seek Him as one Who desires to reward you for your faith-fulness.

STEP 7:

TRUST in God and do not be filled with anxiety. KNOW that He will answer.

*"Do not fret or have any anxiety about any-
thing, but in every circumstance and in everything by prayer and petition [definite requests]
with thanksgiving continue to make your wants
known to God."*

Philippians 4:6 AMP

When we do this, then we are given that wonderful
promise in the next verse: the promise of God's peace,
a peace which passeth understanding.

*"And God's peace [be yours, that tranquil
state of a soul assured of its salvation through
Christ, and so fearing nothing from God and
content with its earthly lot of whatever sort that
is, that peace] which transcends all understanding, shall garrison and mount guard over your
hearts and minds in Christ Jesus."*

AMP

The Message has a very clear and meaningful translation of this passage: *"Don't fret or worry. Instead of
worrying, pray. Let petitions and praises shape your
worries into prayers, letting God know your concerns.
Before you know it, a sense of God's wholeness, everything coming together for good, will come and settle you
down. It's wonderful what happens when Christ dis-
places worry at the center of your life."*[12]

From our experiences I can impress upon you that
this kind of peace and sense of God's wholeness is a
treasure to seek above all others. With this peace from
God you can walk through ANY kind of trial.

From *The Hearing Ear* by Larry Lea:

*Sometimes, even though the word you have
heard in your spirit may line up perfectly with*

the Word of God, it may not be God's will for you or it may not be time to act upon that word. Therefore, learn to let the presence or the absence of the PEACE OF GOD *in your heart be the determining factor. In Colossians 3:15, Paul tells the Colossian believers: 'And let the peace (soul harmony which comes) from the Christ rule (act as umpire continually) in your hearts—deciding and settling with finality all questions that arise in your minds.'*

If you were to receive a word that fills your spirit with peace and causes you to break into spontaneous praise and rejoice, don't be afraid to receive it. Satan and your flesh can speak to you and can even quote scripture, but they cannot counterfeit the peace of God. Peace is a fruit of the Spirit. Satan's "peace" is hollow and phony.[13]

STEP 8:

*"Casting the **whole** of your care—**all** your anxieties, **all** your worries, **all** your concerns, **once and for all**—on Him; for He cares for you affectionately, and cares about you watchfully."*
1 Peter 5:7 AMP

Notice how the Bible is a book of absolutes. We are to cast ALL our worries, cares, and anxieties on Him, and He heals ALL our diseases. We must love Him with ALL our hearts, minds, and souls.

STEP 9:

Obey God. [See Matthew 7:24,25; John 9:31; Exodus 15:26.]

"Praise the Lord! For all who fear God and trust in him are blessed beyond expression. Yes,

*happy is **the man who delights in doing his commands...**Such a man will not be overthrown by evil circumstances.... He does not fear bad news, nor live in dread of what may happen. For he **is settled in his mind that Jehovah will take care of him**.*"

Psalm 112:1,6,7 TLB[14]

"*If you diligently heed the voice of the Lord your God and do what is right in His sight, give ear to His commandments and keep all His statutes, I will put none of the diseases on you which I have brought on the Egyptians. For I am the Lord who heals you.*"

Exodus 15:26

In John 15:10 Jesus further explains, "*If you keep My commandments—if you continue to obey My instructions—you will abide in My love and live on in it; just as I have obeyed My Father's commandments and live on in His love*" (AMP).

"*Delight yourself also in the Lord; and He shall give you the desires of your heart. Commit your way to the Lord. Trust also in Him, and He shall bring it to pass.*"

Psalm 37:4,5

"*...if anyone is a worshiper of God and does His will, He hears him.*"

John 9:31

Anything that God tells us to do is for our own good. Therefore, obedience to His will and to His Word should be what we desire if we really and truly believe Him to be a God of love. We should seek His will from His Word, find the places in our lives where we might

91

have been disobedient, and make corrections. Then His promises can be fulfilled in our lives.

We need to be obedient not from a desire to receive reward but out of a trust in a God who wants what is best for us. Francis de Sales said, "Obedience must rather be loved than disobedience feared."[15] We must get to the point in our lives where we love God so much that His will for us is what we desire more than anything. His plan will become more important than our own selfish wishes or ideas. We will <u>want</u> to obey Him in everything.

One area that applies specifically to health is the concept found in the Bible in 1 Corinthians 3. This scripture speaks of our bodies as being temples of the Spirit. As such they are not to be defiled. Although Paul is speaking to the Church here, we can also realize that when we do things that are hurtful to our bodies, our temples, we are not in the will of our Heavenly Father. This could be putting anything into our bodies that we know can harm them. Many people are in need of control over bad habits that can wreck their health. This can include harmful foods as well as the more obvious health saboteurs such as tobacco, alcohol, and drugs.

STEP 10:

Pray with a heart full of thanksgiving and praise.

> *"Enter into His gates with thanksgiving, and into His courts with praise."*
>
> Psalm 100:4

Many people use thanksgiving and praise as the way to begin praying, to bring them before the throne of God, entering His gates and His courts and then moving on into the Holy of Holies and into His very presence.

First Thessalonians 5:16-18: *"Rejoice always, pray without ceasing, in everything **give thanks**; for this is the will of God in Christ Jesus for you."*

This is another part of letting God know that you are trusting Him **regardless of how things look**. Even **in** illness, we **know** that He is there. **In your heart** (again) you declare your faith in His goodness, thereby giving thanks to Him, the God who will deliver you from whatever bad circumstance you are in.

This is not to say that we have to thank God for the trial itself but for what He can do with the trial as promised in Romans 8:28. All of us have seen the worst kinds of tragedy result in good. The key is to trust in God, remembering that He is a **rewarder** of them who diligently seek Him. Look forward with patience and trust for the fulfillment of His promises. Thanksgiving is a powerful weapon for bringing down Satan's lies.

This kind of faith is not denying reality. It is looking **past** the reality to when God will change it (Romans 4: 17-19).

In addition to thanksgiving, praise is an important weapon of our prayer warfare.

The Bible tells us that God inhabits the praises of His people (Psalm 22:3). Therefore, when we praise Him, He is there with us, a living Presence.

Sometimes in the middle of pain or exhaustion, it is difficult to offer up the praise this verse demands of us. However, we need to make this an act of our will and praise Him even without the emotion being there. This is what God calls the *"sacrifice of praise"* in Hebrews 13:15. It is described further as *"the fruit of our lips, giving thanks to His name."*

It is an act of our **will**. We do it even if we don't feel like it. As the praise rises up in us to God, our spirits will be rewarded with His holy Presence. God will accept our sacrifice, and we will be blessed.

[See also: Philippians 4:6; Colossians 4:2; 1 Thessalonians. 5:16-18.]

STEP 11:

Remember that God's timing is not always our timing. (In fact, it very seldom is.) Persevere! The literal translation of the familiar verse reads: *"**Keep on** asking and it will be given you; **keep on** seeking and you will find; **keep on** knocking [reverently] and the door will be opened to you"* (Matthew 7:7 AMP).

In the book of Hebrews we are cautioned not to throw away the confidence we have built in God's promises. *"Do not, therefore, fling away your fearless confidence, for it carries a great and glorious compensation of reward. For you have need of steadfast patience and endurance, so that you may perform and fully accomplish the will of God, and thus receive and carry away [and enjoy to the full] what is promised* (Hebrews 10:35,36 AMP).

Remember, too, that God doesn't always deliver His children out of the fire, but He ALWAYS walks through the fire with them. His children must learn to be patient as He uses the refining fire of their trials to strengthen them and to make them what He desires them to be. HOLD ON!!! God is faithful to fulfill His promises to you.

STEP 12:

Forgive. Mark 11:25,26 is one of the most difficult passages in the Bible because it tells us that if we do not forgive, then God will not forgive us. Again this demand from God is for our own good. Unforgiveness hardens our hearts. It creates a root of bitterness that the Bible tells us can cause people to turn away from God.

Unforgiveness blocks the avenue for God's blessings to flow down to us. It causes stress and emotional disturbance that can hinder healing.

Charles S. Price says this about forgiveness and healing:

Have you noticed that at the end of the statement our blessed Lord made to His disciples about the faith that would move mountains, He tells them to be sure to forgive everybody against whom they might have some grudge or feeling? Why does He say that in connection with this great lesson on mountain-moving faith? Is it not because of the fact that, when God would impart His faith to us, He does not want to find a channel which is choked by hate and an unforgiving spirit?

...I do not mean to imply that He demands perfection of life and conduct before He imparts the grace of His faith, but perhaps there will be things which He will require of us in order that His blessings He might impart. A God of infinite and eternal love wants no malice in the hearts of His children. How can we, who have been forgiven so much, refuse to forgive those who perchance have transgressed against us?[16]

Neil T. Anderson puts it this way:

> *You don't forgive someone merely for their sake; you do it for your sake so you can be free. Your need to forgive isn't an issue between you and the offender; it's between you and God. Forgiveness is agreeing to live with the consequences of another person's sin. Forgiveness is costly; we pay the price of the evil we forgive. Yet you're going to live with those consequences whether you want to or not; your only choice is whether you will do so in the bitterness of unforgiveness or the freedom of forgiveness.... Forgiveness deals with your pain, not another's behavior.*[17]

Jesus gives us very specific instructions about our treatment of those who trespass against us in Matthew 5:44: *"But I say to you, love your enemies, bless those who curse you, do good to those who hate you, and pray for those who spitefully use you and persecute you."* In the next verse He tells us why: *"that you may be sons of your Father in heaven."*

Isn't being God's child and an heir of all that He has for you worth more to you than holding on to a grudge or holding unforgiveness for another person? Do you really want that person to be a reason that you may not have the fulfillment of all God wants for you?

Although this is a difficult demand of Jesus, He never gives us any command without also providing the grace we will need to carry it out. It is an act of our will just to say and mean it, "God, I am willing." Your honest prayer may have to be, "God, I'm willing to be willing. Help me to **want** to do what You say I must do." God will honor even that much willingness. We forgive others not because of who they are, but because of who **we** are and because of Whom we serve.

I would stress praying for that person. Once you have prayed for a person, his welfare becomes so important to you that the ill feelings cannot stay in the same heart.

Over and over the HEART is the key. We must say with the psalmist: *"Create in me a clean heart, O God, and renew a steadfast spirit within me"* (Psalm 51:10).

To summarize, the conditions for having prayers answered include the following:

1. Sins are confessed and forgiven (Psalm 103).

2. Jesus lives within the person praying (John 15:7).

3. God's words abide in the one praying (John 15:7).

4. The prayer is according to God's will (1 John 5:14,15).

5. The one praying believes in his heart that his prayer will be answered (Mark 11:23,24; Hebrews 11:6; James 1:6).

6. The one praying diligently seeks the will of God, and believes that God will reward him (Hebrews 11:6).

7. The one praying is not anxious or doubtful in his heart (James 1:6; 1 Peter 5:7).

8. The trust of the one praying is totally centered on God, and God is worshipped with ALL the believer's heart, soul, and mind (Psalm 112; Psalm 37:4,5; Jeremiah 29:13; Matthew 22:37).

9. The one praying is obedient and committed to God (Psalm 37:4,5; John 9:31).

10. The prayer is offered in an attitude of worship, praise, and thanksgiving (John 9:31; Philippians 4:6; 1 Thessalonians 5:16-18).

11. The one praying perseveres in his prayer (Luke 11:5-9).

12. The one praying forgives others (Mark 11:25,26).

13. Prayers are offered in the name of Jesus (John 16:23,24).

14. God is glorified through the answer. *"When Jesus heard that, He said, 'This sickness is not unto death, but for the glory of God, that the Son of God may be glorified through it'"* (John 11:4).

"And whatever you ask in My name, that I will do, that the Father may be glorified in the Son" (John 14:13).

Other scriptures where healing led to glorifying God: Mark 2:12; Luke 5:26; Luke 7:16; Luke 18:43.

15. In John 5:6 Jesus asked the sick man, "Do you wish to get well?"

This, too, is one of the main conditions for a person's return to health. Sometimes the "benefits" of being sick may outweigh the reasons for getting better. For example, some people may not want to give up the attention they are receiving or the rest they are finally able to have. They may suffer from guilt and feel the need to suffer. Other psychological reasons may keep a person bound by a disease or an illness. A person needs to examine his heart and see if for any reason he is holding on to his illness.

V

WHEN TO FIGHT

I have observed people in illnesses who have fought to regain their health and others who seem to be resigned to their illness. The results followed as would be expected.

If God's will for us is health, then obviously disease must come either from a breakdown in our immune systems, from our own fleshly desires, or from the devil. If it is a case of the latter, to become well will involve fighting against the devil and refusing every weapon he throws at us.

Even if the sickness itself did not come from the devil, we will need to know how to fight him when he tries to use the sickness to discourage us or to take away our faith.

Jesus healed *"all who were oppressed by the devil."*

Acts 10:38

"Be on the alert. Your adversary, the devil, prowls about like a roaring lion, seeking someone to devour. But resist him, firm in your faith, knowing that...the God of all grace, who called

you... will Himself perfect, confirm, strengthen, and establish you."

1 Peter 5:8-10 NASB

Fight the devil by using God's word against him, just as Jesus did in the wilderness. When doubts creep in, GO BACK TO GOD'S WORD.

To be healed, you fight the devil by quoting healing scriptures. The Word of God defeats the devil every time. Talk **out loud**. Use the name of Jesus when you are rebuking the devil's suggestions. He hates to hear that name and will run from it.

At times when you are weary, you can often use Jesus' name as a prayer. Just say "Jesus" over and over. I promise you from my own dark night's experience that this will work.

Another way to fight the devil is to actively rid our minds of anything that is not legitimately God. The Bible refers to this as *"...bringing every thought into captivity to the obedience of Christ"* (2 Corinthians 10:5).

The devil's stronghold is in your thought life. You must get in the habit of **immediately** taking control over any thought that doesn't line up with God's word. *"Every tongue which rises against you in judgment, YOU shall condemn* [note: or show to be wrong]*"* (Isaiah 54:17). *"This is the heritage of the servants of the Lord,"* continues Isaiah. You must learn to use this power against the devil's scheming thought patterns.

So when messages such as, "I don't have enough faith" or "I'm not worthy" or "God doesn't do all that today" come into your mind, refute them in the name of Jesus. Fight back with a scripture to back up what you have put into your heart. When Satan tries to get into your thoughts, say God's words out loud so that Satan hears them.

We believe in our hearts by an act of our **will**. Our emotions don't always line up with that immediately, so watch out for **feelings**. Remember, the devil can use emotions and feelings, so confess with your mouth what you believe in your heart to fight any emotions that are coming against what you believe for.

> *"For though we walk in the flesh, we do not war according to the flesh, for the weapons of our warfare are not of the flesh, but divinely powerful for the destruction of fortresses. We are destroying speculations and every lofty thing raised up against the knowledge of God, and we are taking every thought captive to the obedience of Christ."*
>
> 2 Corinthians 10:3-5 NASB

I believe that "every lofty thing" refers to our HUMAN reasoning, wisdom, and knowledge (which often will keep us from accepting the supernatural powers of God).

Refuse to allow the devil to have any control over your thoughts. God's Word says that he is a liar. Let him know that you know what he is trying to do. Make the devil see that you believe God more than you believe him, regardless of your circumstances. Jesus set the example for us when He was being tempted by the devil in the wilderness. He used the Word of God to defeat every one of Satan's arguments (Luke 4).

The devil tried more than once to use our sisters' deaths to take away our faith for Don's healing. We would have to remind the devil and to remind ourselves of God's promises. We used scripture to tell him what would be the result. One that we quoted often was Psalm 118:17,18: *"I shall not die, but live, and declare the works of the Lord. The Lord has chastened me severely, but He has not given me over to death."*

"He has delivered us from the power of darkness and conveyed us into the kingdom of the Son of His love" (Colossians 1:13). We are now a part of Jesus' kingdom since we have been saved. Nothing from the devil's kingdom then should be a part of our lives. Therefore, we are to reject anything the devil tries to put into our kingdom position with Jesus.

"If anyone does attack you, it will not be my doing," says the Lord in Isaiah 54:15 NIV. Fear is an emotion that attacks people in illness. However, this fear, although natural in the human sphere, is NOT from God. Throughout the Bible God commands us to "Fear not." [See Isaiah 54:14; Deuteronomy 31:8; Isaiah 43:1,2; Isaiah 41:13.] Second Timothy 1:7 says, *"God has not given us a spirit of fear, but of power and of love and of a sound mind."*

Isaiah also reminds us, *"No weapon formed against you shall prosper"* (Isaiah 54:17). Listen to the original Hebrew translation of this verse: *"No plan, no instrument of destruction, no satanic artillery shall push you or run over you, but it will be done away with."*

Jesus Himself gives us power over Satan's attacks: *"Behold, I give you the authority to trample on serpents and scorpions, and over all the power of the enemy, and nothing shall by any means hurt you"* (Luke 10:19). The footnotes of the *Spirit-Filled Life Bible* state, *"Serpents and scorpions are symbols of spiritual enemies and*

demonic power, over which Jesus has given His follow-
ers power."[18]

God has promised to help us wreck Satan's attacks. *"We are more than conquerors through Him who loved us"* (Romans 8:37). We are not to sit back and let the devil take advantage of our weakness.

Look at the words in these scriptures:

weapon, conquerors
adversary, captive
rise up against you
weapons of warfare
destruction of fortresses
power of darkness
divinely powerful
resist, trample
ATTACK

None of these are passive words. We have to realize that we are in a WAR, and we have to fight to win. You have to play an ACTIVE role in your battle.

SEEK God constantly.
UNITE yourself to Jesus.
STUDY God's Word. PRAISE God.
WORSHIP God. WITNESS for Him.
FIGHT the devil by quoting God's Word.

These are all action verbs. "God doesn't DO His will in your life. He does what you LET Him do" (Hugh Smith).

Put on the armor of God and FIGHT the devil, believing and knowing that God is by your side, fighting with you. This is not to take away what I said earlier about resting in God. That kind of rest is an internal rest and a total security of KNOWING that GOD IS IN CONTROL. It is not passivity and acceptance of "whatever life gives me." It is being in submission to God that leads to total trust. This total trust gives His peace.

"Therefore submit to God. Resist the devil and he will flee from you. Draw near to God, and He will draw near to you" (James 4:7,8). When we submit, we can rest in His power and in the assurance that **He** will take care of the situation. Then with that power in us, we can actively resist the devil. Note the order of these two actions. First we must submit to God. Without that submission we do not have the power we need to fight Satan.

REMEMBER ALWAYS: *"Greater is He who is in you than he who is in the world* (Satan)*"* (1 John 4:4 NASB).

Satan has no more power than you do if Jesus is in you!!!!

Jesus said, *"With men this is impossible, but WITH GOD ALL THINGS ARE POSSIBLE"* (Matthew 19:26).

Be a channel for God's power to work through you.

A very important caution from *The Hearing Ear* by Larry Lea:

> *If you have a spiritual experience that does not line up with the person, nature, and character of Jesus Christ, rebuke it and leave it alone because it is of the devil. If you receive a message that does not agree perfectly with the Word of God, disregard it because God never contradicts His Word. [See Psalm 119:4, 5;24.]...If it brings confusion, condemnation, or discouragement, disregard the word because it didn't come from God. [See 1 Corinthians 14:33 and James 3:15.]*[19]

VI

A NOTE OF ENCOURAGEMENT

What does "through the fire" suggest to you? Is the fire we walked through the illness itself? The treatment? The surgeries? The emotions? The doubt?

Yes, it is all of these. However, one of the nurses at CTCT wrote to us and said, "We all know that the fire is the fear."

And for a person facing a terminal illness, the primary fire IS the fear. Once you can get past the fear, everything else becomes easier.

Fear is an emotion that attacks people when they are ill: fear of the unknown, fear of the treatment and side effects, fear of pain, fear of death, fear of how the illness will affect loved ones. This fear is natural in the human sphere of the unknown, but we have to remember that fear is NOT from God.

Second Timothy 1:7 says, *"God has not given us a spirit of fear, but of power and of love and of a sound mind."*

Fear is a weapon used by Satan to make us give up our kingdom position in Christ Jesus, especially when we are in a weakened state as we are when fighting an illness. God tells us in Isaiah 54:15 NIV, *"If anyone does attack you, it will not be my doing."* So when paralyzing fear attacks you, you must remember that your enemy is coming against you, not your Father. Also remember that the spirit within you is greater than the enemy and his weapons (1 John 4:4).

Isaiah 54:17 reminds us, *"No weapon formed against you shall prosper."* In the original Hebrew translation, *"No plan, no instrument of destruction, no satanic artillery shall push you or run over you, but it will be done away with."*

Isaiah goes on to say, *"...and every tongue which rises against you in judgment you shall condemn."* Notice that in this scripture God gives US the power to condemn Satan's attack of fear. Jesus reiterated this in Luke 10 when He said, *"I give you the authority to trample on serpents and scorpions, and over all the power of the enemy, and nothing shall by any means hurt you."*

According to Biblical scholars, *serpents* and *scorpions* here are symbols of spiritual enemies and demonic power (satanic artillery). Fear is perhaps the biggest spiritual weapon or demonic power that Satan throws at people when they are faced with a life-threatening situation. We need to be reminded that we have been given power over this enemy of fear.

"We are more than conquerors through Him who loved us" (Romans 8:37).

Remember from our stories how God took away Carol's fear of dying, how Don faced his diagnosis with, "That word doesn't scare me. Our God is bigger than cancer." Recall how He blessed me with the absence of fear. He will do the same for you.

The opposite of fear is peace. I believe that there are five steps that will get a person from fear to peace. These have been covered in the book, but I'd like to just outline them here for you so that you can see the progression.

What are the steps from fear to peace?

1. Know God's character.
2. Know His love.
3. This knowledge of Him will lead to total trust in Father.
4. Trust leads to relinquishment.
5. Relinquishment leads to joy (real joy—the gift of the Spirit—that does not depend upon circumstances)....
6. .... and on into PEACE and REST.

Know God's character. How? God's character is found in His Word, and crisis drives us to His Word. Exhaustive studies have been done on the character of God. One that I highly recommend is Kay Arthur's book *Lord, I Want To Know You*, a study on the names of God, which reflect His character and explain who He is.

I have already shared much of what I know about our Father. Second Corinthians 1:3 calls Him *"the Father of mercies and God of all comfort."* Hebrews 11:6 reminds us that God is *"a rewarder of those who diligently seek Him."* God's character is seen throughout the Bible. He is the Creator, the God who sees, the all-sufficient one. He is our provider, our healer, our righteousness, our shepherd, our sanctifier, our deliverer, our peace. He is everything we need and exactly what we need at any given point in our lives. To show all that God is would require another book.

I encourage you to make it your daily goal to find out all you can about the character of your Father. Get into the Word, and let God show you who He is and how much He cares for you.

Know God's love. You need to conceive as best you can how much Father loves you. In his letter to the Ephesians Paul prayed that they would "*understand... how wide, how long, how high, and how deep [God's] love really is.*" He prayed that they would experience the love of Christ, *though it is so great you will never fully understand it*" (Ephesians 3:18,19 NLT).

First John 4:18 tells us that perfect love casts out fear. Of course, the only perfect love is the love God has for His children. You can experience and feel this awesome love and let it cast your fear away.

When describing faith, hope, and love, Paul determines that the greatest of these is love. One reason that love is the greatest is because you have to have knowledge of God's love before you can have hope.

When you have heart knowledge of Father God's faithfulness and His love, then you KNOW that you can trust Him. Job 11:18 says, "*You would be secure because there is hope.*" Once that hope is established in your heart because you know His love, then your anxiety vanishes. You are secure. You are confident. You feel totally safe. You have taken the third step.

When your heart is settled so that you trust Father completely, then you come to the most important step you can make in getting past your fears and into peace. That step is the step of relinquishment. Once you recognize your helplessness and hopelessness without God and you come to the end of your own efforts, you may cry out, "I can't do this." Once you get to that point, then you can rejoice. Because you have focused on His love, you know that although you can't do it, YOUR FATHER CAN. You are fully ready to give it all over to Him.

You are not giving up. You are, as Glenn Clark explains it, giving over. *"You are giving yourself completely into the hands of the Father to do whatever He knows is best for you. Trust Him completely, utterly, perfectly."*

I was able to relinquish Don to God the night that I heard His voice assuring me that He could take care of the tumors. Because I had been in the Word, learning of His character, I knew that I could lean on Him with abandonment. I readily gave my husband's situation up into the hands of a loving, perfect Father. Don relinquished the situation to God when his heart was stirred by the faith of the Hebrews who walked through the fire, believing in their God to deliver them in His own way. In his heart he said, "You do it Your way, Father God. I trust You completely."

After you give over to God and trust Him to accomplish His purposes in His way, then you can have joy even in the midst of your crisis. James 1:2-4 says for us to *"count it all joy"* when trouble comes our way because troubles strengthen us to be ready for anything. When Habakkuk said that he would rejoice in the Lord, everything was wrong externally for him. Yet he was able to say, *"I will JOY in the God of my salvation"* (Habakkuk 3:18). The word *joy* as used here means *to dance or leap for joy.* Obviously Habakkuk KNEW and TRUSTED his God and could give all of his problems over to Him with joyfulness, regardless of outward circumstances.

Nehemiah 8:10 reminds us that the joy of the Lord is our strength. So rejoice in the Lord. Keep those endorphins working. Remember all of the joyful experiences Don and I had during some of our bleakest reports? This strength was not our own. It was the Lord's, given to us because we knew Him as a loving, faithful Father whom we could trust.

Remember Paul's exhortation to the Philippians: *"Always be full of joy in the Lord. I say it again—rejoice!...Don't worry about anything; instead pray about everything. Tell God what you need, and thank Him for all He has done."* Notice what follows when we do this: *"If you do this, you will experience God's peace, which is far more wonderful than the human mind can understand. His peace will guard your hearts and minds as you live in Christ Jesus"* (Philippians 4:4,6,7 NLT).

Or as *The Amplified Bible* says it: *"And God's peace [be yours, that tranquil state of a soul assured of its salvation through Christ, and so fearing nothing from God and content with its earthly lot of whatever sort that is, that peace] which transcends all understanding, shall garrison and mount guard over your hearts and minds in Christ Jesus"* (v.7).

So then you are at step six, and what a blessed place to be! You have the peace that passes all understanding. You have been freed from paralyzing fear and have passed into a position of security and total assurance that a loving God has you in His hands.

Covering every one of these steps is the grace of God. There is no way that any of us can get to His peace unless He gives us His grace. But the wonderful truth of it all is that God never asks us to do anything without equipping us to do it. Someone has said that the letters in *grace* represent God's Requirements And Christ's Enablement. Whatever He tells us to do, He enables us to do it. God tells us to have faith and bestows His faith to us, to hope in Him and gives us His hope, to count it all joy and gives us His joy, to fear not and gives us His peace. We never have to depend upon our own resources. We just have to ask for and accept His resources and then wait on Him to complete the work.

Know God's character. Experience His love. Have total trust in Him as your Father. Relinquish all to Him. Rejoice in the Lord. Enter into His peace and rest. Leave your fear behind you and walk in God's peace.

In the book of Ephesians, Paul prays a beautiful prayer of encouragement over the people. Please consider this our prayer over you:

I pray to the Father, the Creator of everything in heaven and on earth...that from his glorious, unlimited resources he will give you mighty inner strength through his Holy Spirit. And I pray that Christ will be more and more at home in your hearts as you trust in him. May your roots go down deep into the soil of God's marvelous love. And may you have the power to understand, as all God's people should, how wide, how long, how high, and how deep his love really is. May you experience the love of Christ, though it is so great you will never fully understand it. Then you will be filled with the fullness of life and power that comes from God...He is able to accomplish infinitely more than we would ever dare to ask or hope (Ephesians 3:14-20 NLT).[20]

OTHER ENCOURAGING SCRIPTURES

2 Corinthians 4:16-18
Psalm 91
Matthew 7:9-11
Matthew 7:24-27
Psalm 139
Jeremiah 29:11-13
John 14:10-21
Ephesians 3:14-21
Psalm 130
Deuteronomy 30:11-20
Psalm 18
Psalm 37:7
Proverbs 24:3-6,13,14
Psalm 56
Romans 15:4
Job 11:18
1 Samuel 17:45-47
Psalm 112:6,7
Psalm 119:25,49-72
Psalm 1:21
Romans 8:31-39

Endnotes

1. Source unknown.
2. Patsy Clairmont, *Normal Is Just a Setting on Your Dryer* (Colorado Springs, Colorado: Family Publishers, 1993).
3. Dawn Thomas, "He'll Do It Again" (Do-Dat Music Publishers, Franklin, Tennessee). Used by permission.
4. Gloria Gaither, Sandi Patti, and Phil McHugh, "In the Name of the Lord" (Gaither Music Co., Sandi's Songs Music and River Oaks Music, 1986). Used by permission.
5. David Wilkerson, *Hungry for More of Jesus* (Grand Rapids, Michigan: Chosen Books, a division of Baker Book House Company, 1992), pp. 84-94. Used by permission.
6. Charles S. Price, *The Real Faith* (South Plainfield, New Jersey: Bridge-Logos Publishers, 1972), pages 71,74,79,85. Used by permission.
7. Price, p. 96.
8. Anne E. Frahm, *A Cancer Battle Plan* (Colorado Springs, Colorado: Pinion, 1992).
9. Patrick Quillan, *Beating Cancer with Nutrition* (Tulsa, Oklahoma: The Nutrition Times Press, Inc., 1994).
10. *Spirit-Filled Life Bible* (Nashville, Tennessee: Thomas Nelson, Inc.), p. 1471.
11. Price, p. 69.
12. *The Message* (Colorado Springs, Colorado: Nav Press, 1993).
13. Larry Lea, *The Hearing Ear* (Lake Mary, Florida: Creation House, 1988), pp. 160-161. Used by permission.

14. *The Living Bible* (Wheaton, Illinois: Tyndale House Publishers, 1971).
15. Gary Thomas, *Seeking the Face of God* (Nashville, Tennessee: Thomas Nelson, 1994), p. 54. Used by permission.
16. Price, pp. 54,55.
17. Neil T. Anderson, *The Bondage Breaker* (Eugene, Oregon: Harvest House, 1990), pp. 195,197. Used by permission.
18. *Spirit-Filled Life Bible*, p. 1533.
19. Lea, p. 160.
20. *The New Living Translation* (Wheaton, Illinois: Tyndale House Publishers, Inc., 1996).

RECOMMENDED READING

F. F. Bosworth, *Christ the Healer* (Grand Rapids, Michigan: Baker Book House Company, 1973).

Max Lucado, *He Still Moves Stones* (Dallas, Texas: Word Publishing, 1993).

Jan Markell, *Waiting for a Miracle* (Grand Rapids, Michigan: Baker Books, 1993).

Charles S. Price, *The Real Faith for Healing,* edited and rewritten (New Brunswick, New Jersey: Bridge Logos, Publishers, 1997).

Gwen Wilkerson, *In His Strength* (Glendale, California: Regal Books Division, G/L Publications, 1978).

Kay Arthur, *Lord, I Want to Know You* (Colorado Springs, Colorado: Waterbrook Press, 1992).